INVISIBLE DUBLIN

INVISIBLE DUBLIN

A Journey Through
Dublin's Suburbs

Edited by Dermot Bolger

Raven Arts Press

Invisible Dublin
is first published in 1991 by
The Raven Arts Press
P.O. Box 1430
Finglas
Dublin 11
Ireland

ISBN 1 85186 089 4

Raven Arts Press receives financial support from
The Arts Council (An Chomhairle Ealaíon), Dublin, Ireland.

Acknowledgements are made to *The Sunday Tribune* where Gene
Kerrigan's article first appeared, to The Attic Press where Nell
McCafferty's article was published in *Goodnight Sisters* – Volume
Two of her Selected Writings, and to *Magill* where an earlier
version of Eamon Dunphy's article first appeared.

Cover photo by Tony O'Shea. Cover design and inside design by
Rapid Productions. Printed and bound in Dublin by Colour
Books Ltd., Baldoyle.

Editor's Note

In 1988 Raven Arts published *Invisible Cities*, an anthology of poetry and prose (with photographs by Podge O'Farrell) which took the form of a journey through the suburbs of Dublin. Although a success, it fell between two stools with both booksellers and reviewers, neither seemingly sure whether to treat it as a collection of poems or essays. In deciding to reissue it, we have chosen to retain the original twelve essays and commission another fourteen, and to leave the poetry to perhaps in turn be expanded into a separate anthology at a later date.

Under the title, *Invisible Dublin*, and as part of The Raven Collection, we are proud to release it as a unique record of a journey starting with Ferdia MacAnna's Howth, and the Raheny of Sara Berkeley and Hilary Fannin, through such times and places (to mention only a few) as Paul Kimmage's Coolock, June Considine's and Podge Rowan's Finglas, the Crumlin of Fintan O'Toole, the Ballyfermot of Noel McFarlane, the various Tallaghts of Kieran Fagan, Annette Halpin, Leland Bardwell and Heather Brett and on to the Dundrum of Eavan Boland to finish in Joe Jackson's Glasthule.

I hope it is a journey the reader finds full of recognition, contradiction and discovery.

CONTENTS:

For my father and in memory of my mother,
a Wexford lad and a Monaghan girl,
two new Dubliners.

INTRODUCTION

From the old offices of a forgotten newspaper, *The Evening Mail*, later set ablaze by glue sniffers, down a ramshackle laneway in the derelict centre of the old city of Dublin, each day in the year of 1983, I set out in a battered blue van to bring books to the often invisible cities of a new Dublin. To my right, as I crossed the tarmacadamed yard, workmen on scaffolds constructing the Municipal bunkers over the Viking remains of Wood Quay, wolf-whistled down at the girls. The vans nosed their way into the congested traffic, climbed up by the dwarfed Cathedral and were gone on their journeys into the half-built hearts of our new cities.

Working on those draughty mobile libraries, it often seemed that on many of the stops we were like frontier troops, a token advance party sent from the heart of a crumbling city awash with folksy nostalgia and rotting buildings out into the new worlds, the colonies of children and cement tucked away in the distance. I remember the sensation of a crowd waiting in the darkness, swarming over the flattened mud beside a half finished road as the van pulled in to Jobstown or Killinarden, the frenzy of a Friday night in Springfield, the surreal quality of Rivermeath – a tiny isolated estate perched among North Dublin fields as if dropped there from the claws of a giant bird. On many days we were bound for quiet settled suburban oases – the Green at Cypress Grove, Palmerstown, Ballybrack and Doddsborough in Lucan. Or else we wandered through the overgrown lanes of Fingal, to Loughshinny with its tiny harbour, the isolated village of Naul where the great Finglas born piper, Seamus Ennis, lived out his last days in a caravan, or the winter darkness of Corballis Crossroads in Donabate where the sea could be glimpsed whitely in the distance and an

11

old and fiercely intelligent woman with the most beautiful name I had ever heard, Lucinda Isabella Bright, walked to us out of the blackness and often accepted a lift to her home across the golf course on the back of a neighbour's tractor.

I grew to know and love Dublin in all its diversity, and yet it is the strange world of those new housing estates that remains most vividly in my head. In the small shopping centre where we parked in Neilstown, the apathetic and haphazard planning was summed up by the fact that one of the two large signs proclaiming the placename spelled it *Neilstown* and the other *Neillstown*.

I, too, had been born in such an invisible place – a country village populated by an influx of families from both the old city and the country, all in search of *Lebensraum*.

My family and most of my street were the country ones, retaining their habits, their customs, and, even after decades, their accents. As my sister June describes in this book, we woke to the sound of chickens in a long row of gardens that, at night, foxes still crept along streets of concrete to reach. A few streets away children who had run down the corridors of tenement houses now chased plastic balls along roads where cars were rarely seen. Both of us were equally displaced, us in our purchased houses, them in their corporation ones, our strengths being united together and then divided into Residents' and Tenants' Associations.

This was neither country nor city – these streets possessed no place in the school books and poems we learnt at our wooden desks.

It seemed to take years for the media to discover the world of Finglas and when they did it was to report on things that, while still occurring occasionally there, had long since moved their centre elsewhere, to newer suburbs, newer groups of displaced peoples who had not yet bonded together.

In that summer of 83, I published a book called *Lutheran Letters* by the Italian writer and film director Pier Paolo Pasolini. Shortly before his murder in 1975, he entitled one of his Letters *Outside the Palace*. Studying a newspaper on a beach

12

in Ostia he begins to understand that both the people who write for the paper and those whom they write about live "within the Palace". Therefore "there is not a page, not a line... in all the dailies and weeklies in which so many pages are given over to the news which does not refer solely and exclusively to what goes on *in the Palace*.

Only what goes on *in the Palace* seems worthy of attention and interest; all the rest is minutiae, a swarming mass, shapeless, second-rate."

According to Pasolini the Palace consisted of "the lives of the most powerful people there, those who occupy the peaks of power. To be 'serious' means, apparently, to be concerned with these people, their intrigues, their alliances, their conspiracies, their strokes of luck, and finally, *also*, with the way in which they interpret the reality that exists *outside the Palace* - that boring reality which, in the last analysis everything depends on, even if it is unsmart and unserious to bother with it."

On those days in that year when I rode those vans through acres of muck and packed for lunch among the miles of abandoned cars and caravans that border parts of the city, I began to see, more and more, the same Palace reflected in most of the newspapers I read; in the way in which the placenames they were now discovering were a decade out of date; in the strange reality, of which there was nothing folksy, of those parts of Clondalkin and Tallaght, of the staggering mass of Blanchardstown and beyond, and of the estates cast adrift in the fields of North Dublin. And I suspected it was always this way, that the real news - not the stances and stale rhetoric of politicians which frequently led the bulletins, but the extraordinary battles and courage of people who took on the frequently inhospitable landscapes they inherited from planners and builders and, despite everything, survived to establish living places – that this real news always happened off screen, ignored by most of the media who would not finally catch up until years later.

When the Palace did attempt to describe the city outside

their own walls, it was frequently in hopelessly convenient and outdated terms. The myth remained that the city was exclusively divided between poor and uncouth Northsiders and rich and sophisticated Southsiders. While it is certainly the case that the Southside does contain more inhabitants in the higher income brackets than the Northside – even allowing for what – if they were poor – would be referred to as the ghettoes of Howth and Sutton, the reality – and it has been so for at least two decades – is that there is equally as many people living on low incomes South of the Liffey as their counterparts across the river. But the Palace's image of the city was as if somebody had come along with a bottle of Tipp-ex and discreetly removed all Southside human life not attached to a dart station. The vast enclaves of Tallaght, of Clondalkin, of Crumlin, of Ballyfermot, the slopes of Rathfarnham reaching out to the mountains, the Fatima Mansions and The Dolphin's Barns which geographically would not fit into the idea of the Northside and socially would not fit into the Palace's vision of The Southside were simply presumed not to exist in this definition.

In Kieran Fagan's fine essay in this book about living in Tallaght, he describes how the media often turn their attention to Tallaght, firstly by ignoring the reality that eighty thousand ordinary people live ordinary lives there as "this is not the stuff of great columns or searing TV documentaries, pithy, passionate and committed, about the deprivations suffered by unfortunates 'living out in Tallaght'." And secondly, when their editors realise that their "suburban sprawl without a soul" stories have brought a tide of rank ingratitude down on their heads, by bathing the population of Tallaght in a follow up piece with "Community Spirit". As Fagan remarks "Of all the insults ever visited on the long-suffering people of south west Dublin, this has to be the worst. To be covered with this syrupy confection, this sticky fictional goo laid all over our downtrodden lives, just because A Great Thinker got it wrong first time around, is more than flesh and blood should have to bear.."

Yet if the Palace chose to mainly ignore life in the suburbs where the vast majority of people lived, many sections of it (along with those who are frequently systematically destroying what is left of the old city) have helped to keep alive the myth of 'the true Dub.' The man whose great-great-great grandad had walked the cobbled streets, worked the ancient city trades and probably even — if current historical research on her sideline occupations is to be believed - contracted nefarious social diseases from Molly Malone.

The danger of this folksy nostalgia is that it has helped create the illusion that somehow the real Dublin is dead, the real Dubliners scattered or dying out and that some alien city is rising in its place. During the Millennium celebrations, when the first version of this book was published, they issued commemorative postcards of the Strawberry Beds as it was a half century before while at the same time starting work on the motorway flyover that would completely change the Strawberry Beds' character. If the present reality is so awful that we have to paper it over with postcards of the past, then we should not be making these changes. Or if these changes are for the good then we should not be ashamed to celebrate them as part of a living city.

Because the greatest aspect of Dublin is not its buildings or history but the fact that it is a living city. A city is like a person, it is always changing. Nobody has the right to lay special claim to it. The Vietnamese boat person living in Clondalkin has as much right to feel part of it as somebody whose family has lived in the same inner city street for a century. A city, by its nature, is comprised of migrants and the children and grandchildren of migrants. Dublin — like the country it is capital of — has a blessedly bastardised population with each generation providing its new influx of fresh blood and vitality. To me, at least, if the awful term 'a real Dubliner' has to be used, then it is anyone who has been born or has chosen to live there and now regards the city as his or her home, and the real Dublin is wherever they stake their claim to that home.

Rather than being dead it is alive and vibrant with new people, with new blood, new streets, new placenames. Its history is not finished but yet to be written by the masses of children who are still living it. This anthology is, in some small way, an attempt to chronicle the lives of Dublin people as it has been lived by them in the Dublin of today.

By its nature, it can only be a short journey, leaving out far more places and experiences than it can take in. Some areas of the city which have been more than amply chronicled before have been left out in my attempts to take in as much of the new and often rootless areas which have grown up - areas where often, as in the cases here of Paul Kimmage in Coolock and Joe Jackson in Glasthule, one was advised not to even put down the name of the place you were from when writing letters. Other areas simply, as yet, do not have people to speak for them. In the same way as the authors of this book have attempted, through writing of their own experiences, to describe the city of the 1960s, 70s and 80s, it will be those people growing to maturity now who will eventually be the true chroniclers of the Dublin city of the 1990s.

It may take to the end of the century for somebody to shape such a volume and even then, as the next generation attempt their own definition, their children will hopefully be exploring new streets, and creating new myths and heroes beyond their parents' comprehension, as the real history and the real news goes on being created away from the turned-in eyes *inside the Palace*.

Dermot Bolger,
Finglas.

HOMETOWN
Ferdia Mac Anna

I was five when we moved to Howth. The new house was a whitewashed bungalow near the summit. It was a lot different to the rented flat in Pearse Street. From our front porch, I could see the bumpy green fields sloping down to the blue sea and Ireland's Eye beyond. The air was so sharp it hurt to take a deep breath. It was like living on the top of the world.

Beyond the back garden, across the rolling fields of gorse and heather, was a hill of broken rocks that looked ideal for war games. Everywhere was green and wild. It made me want to put on sneakers and run.

Best of all, there was a rusted roller in the front garden that I could flatten things with.

After a day or two, the local kids came around to check out my sister and me.

"Where're you from?", one asked me.

"We come from The High Kings", I answered according to my mother's instructions.

The kids were not impressed. One girl told me she was going to ask around and find out. She was sure we were from Cabra.

The next day, my mother sent me up the road to the newsagents at the summit to buy cigarettes and matches. In the shop doorway, a skinny, fair-haired boy with a sharp face blocked my way. He was the first boy I'd ever seen who was as tall as me.

"Give me twopence, or I'll burst you", he said.

I wouldn't give him twopence. So he burst me. I ran home crying.

A few days later, the boy grew tired of trouncing me. We became friends instead. He told me his name was Nessan and that his people had lived in Howth for hundreds of years.

Nessan and I formed a gang and hung around the shops demanding twopences from the other kids. Nobody took any heed of our threats and there didn't seem to be any point bursting people for nothing. So we gave up the protection racket and turned to more healthy pursuits, such as football, robbing orchards, playing cowboys, and shoving cow-pats from the fields through people's letterboxes before running off.

By the time we were eleven we had our own bicycle gang called, with great solemnity, The Howth Bikers. For dares, we cycled at top speed along dangerous cliff walks and rattly back paths. Our biggest kick was to freewheel down the hill of Howth to the town without using brakes. Some guys managed the feat with their arms folded – they steered with their feet on the handlebars.

It was dangerous. But it was a lot more fun than giving wrong directions to the American tourists who were always cruising the hill in their smart rented cars, looking for The Abbey Tavern.

In the early sixties, Howth still had a relatively small population. Those from the small fishing-town rarely mixed with the hill-dwellers. Howth folk referred to all new arrivals as "runners". Later, I found out that anyone whose Howth roots didn't go back at least a century was a "runner". It was a close-knit community. Not unfriendly, just clannish.

But even outside the town there was a distance between households. Howth hill was a private, mysterious place – there were mansions that never seemed to have any lights on at night, black-windowed Mercedes that zoomed past, and snooty kids who wouldn't talk to you no matter what you said. Even the dogs were too cool to be petted.

There was rarely any excitement. Except in the summers when the gorse-fires broke out.

It didn't take the kids long to discover that you got ten bob for reporting a gorse fire. Every summer, there would be an epidemic. Until the Fire Brigade got wise to the fact that the same kids were showing up at each fire to claim the ten bob reward.

The practice ceased only when one of the gangs had a narrow escape: they had just set fire to a big field of gorse when the wind changed suddenly, forcing them to leg it for their lives. After that, most of the kids thought it safer to get summer jobs.

In our early teens though, none of us had a summer job. We spent the bright, clear days hanging out at the summit, or lolling about in the back fields listening to Radio Caroline on Nessan's brother Michael's transistor. The Beatles, The Who, The Small Faces. Gary Puckett and The Union Gap, and Creedence were our favourites. The Stones were shams. Herman's Hermits were a bunch of lilies.

When we were feeling really bored, we walked down to Jameson's beach on the Sutton side of the cliffs. We sat on the white pebbles with all our clothes on, staring at the bikinied girls.

One day, walking along the cliff path, we spied a couple making love on a private strand far below. We hid in the tall grass and watched until they were finished. They were too far away for us to make out exactly what was going on. But we could see the sunlight glinting on the man's bare arse, so we knew it was something dirty.

The incident inspired us to learn all we could about sex. We sneaked up on young lovers whenever we found them canoodling in tall grass along the cliff walks. We figured we'd pick up a few tips, or get a good chase. We got more chases than tips.

We played soccer on the green outside the pub. There was never any time limit. Players would play for a couple of hours, then get called home for their dinner, then resume playing until teatime or until it got too dark to see the ball. One seven-a-side match lasted all day and ended 49-48.

Sometimes, we played with the Big Blokes who always tried to impress us. Butts from Stella Maris put on goalkeeping exhibitions. After each acrobatic dive he'd puff out his cheeks and blow to show he'd just made the save of the season.

Little Frankie from the summit was so tough nobody would

tackle him. He saw himself as Howth's Jimmy Greaves and liked to give a running commentary on his own performance: "...and the ball comes to Gree-aves, he beats one man, a-nudder, he shoots, WAAAAAH...it's a brilliant go-al. Just listen to that fuckin' crowd". He gave the same commentary when he missed, which was most of the time.

The local superstar was Nessan's brother Jesse, who played for Howth Celtic. On a good day he made us all look like goalposts.

Everyone looked forward to the fights, which usually happened when one side was losing badly. Once a fight broke out, all those not involved would sit on the wall outside the pub to watch.

Big John liked to pick on me. I was four years younger than him, but taller. That made him mad. From the age of six, I was beaten up by Big John at least three times a year. It became a ritual.

One afternoon, when I was thirteen, I challenged Big John to a duel. We met in the middle of secluded Wingate Lane, just opposite my house. To give myself an edge, I carried our wooden clothesline pole behind my back. It stuck up behind me like a lance. When Big John saw it he roared.

While he was still laughing, I hit him over the head with the pole. He fell to the ground. I dropped the pole and jumped on him. For a few glorious moments, I sat on top of him, rubbing his face into the gravel and pounding on his head with my puny fists – just as he had done to me so many times. When Big John recovered he beat the crap out of me.

I went home bruised and crying, but feeling triumphant. My opponent had a black eye and a bloody gash on his lip. Later, I had my allowance stopped for losing the family clothesline pole, but it was worth it. Big John never beat me up again.

That Christmas, there was a blizzard. Howth summit was completely cut off. Not even a land rover or snow plough could get up the hill. For four days, every kid on the hill was out throwing snowballs at every adult who dared to venture out. We attacked shops, the local pub, private houses, even the nuns who lived in a monastery at the Bailey. The nuns were the only ones who didn't return fire.

For transport, we hijacked sheets of corrugated iron from the building sites and used them as sleds. We hit crazy, exhilarating speeds down the deserted, snowy roads.

When the roads cleared, we hid in the hedges at the summit and ambushed cars, buses and cyclists. One driver got out to fight us, but his car slid away on the sleety ground. He had to chase it half a mile down Thormanby Road before he could jump in.

Our bungalow was always full of noise and people. You could never tell what was going to happen next. We'd come from school to find old Republicans in the kitchen, warbling on about Pearse and 1916 and giving out about the Brits.

Sometimes, there were famous writers asleep in our beds, or celebrated actors telling tales in the front room. People mysteriously showed up, stayed with us for weeks and then disappeared abruptly, never to be mentioned again. Once, I came home to find the Russian ambassador drinking whiskey with my mother on the porch.

Things usually calmed down when my father came home from work and sat in his favourite dark, squeaky leather chair by the fire. But when my father was away directing plays or lecturing in U.S. colleges, his kids ran wild. My mother often spent her time waging war on the neighbours, or phoning the government to complain about the way the country was going. Whenever we were out playing, we'd know dinner was ready when we saw the black plume of smoke rising from the back of our house.

One Christmas, my mother put mint sauce on the plum pudding. Everyone ate it and complimented the cook. That was the last time we had guests for Christmas dinner.

My brother Niall and I went to school in the city. Each morning we waited at the bus stop across the road for the little red single-decker to take us down to the train station by the harbour. One driver – a red faced, gap-toothed baldy – terrified everyone on the hill. If you didn't have the correct fare he'd put you off and make you walk. It was ten years before I heard him say "good morning" to anyone, and then it was only because he was due to retire and scared of losing his pension.

The girls in Howth were too cool to even smile. At the local hops in Sutton Tennis club or Suttonians Rugby club, they sat around and ignored requests to dance. They were above all that stuff. If a boy wanted to get off with one of them he had to come up with a really good angle, or throw a really good party.

When I was sixteen, I threw my first "free house". My parents had gone away for a night, so I invited all my friends to stay over. All the local teenagers turned up, too. Everyone got drunk on cider and beer. It was a great social success, even though everyone concerned was too legless to get off with anyone.

After that, my sister and I threw "free houses" whenever my parents went away. The parties became the local disgrace. The neighbours called us "The Wild Mac Annas".

One night, the police were called. There were over a hundred teenagers in the house, scattered throughout the various tiny rooms. Some had even brought their own portable record players. The police insisted on interviewing everyone, on the doorstep. They also wanted the music switched off. But each time a record was yanked off a turntable, another could be heard playing in a different room.

When the police finally gave up and went away, there was still rock music baying from one of the bedrooms as well as a bunch of people hiding in the back garden.

Early next morning, my parents arrived home unexpectedly. As my father walked up the drive, a hundred people including me were exiting the house through the back door and windows, sprinting up the back garden, and vaulting the back wall to take off across the fields.

After that, "Free Houses" didn't seem such a good idea anymore.

That Easter, a fog descended on Howth. It got so bad that cars drove at walking pace. At night, most people stayed indoors.

To relieve the boredom, we stole three dozen eggs from one of the local shops and formed The Great Easter Egg Gang. Then we roamed the hill, launching egg attacks at the windows of the rich folks. Some eggs exploded against the glass like grenades, causing the people inside to leap out of their chairs. One family erupted from their dinner table, tossing knives and forks and plates in the air. They stared out into the fog with wide, jittery eyes. All they saw was yellow yolk slithering down their windowpane.

The Egg Gang became the talk of Howth. For three nights we terrorised the neighbourhood. Police cars cruised the mists searching for us, but we dodged them without bother.

On the fourth night the fog lifted. We decided to quit while we were ahead. Another gang embarked that evening on their own egg crusade, but were easily caught. The unlucky bunch got the blame for all our misdeeds.

After the Leaving Cert, I was convinced that I was now a Big Bloke. But the real Big Blokes still didn't treat me as an equal. I couldn't figure out what the problem was; I had just left school, I smoked Major, I drank pints of Guinness in the town pubs just as they did. I even had a packet of Durex which I kept in the top pocket of my denim jacket – just in case.

My first steady girlfriend was a Canadian tourist named Rose. She and I went for walks along the cliffs. It was a week before I found the courage to lead her into one of the secluded spots. But the romantic interlude was a disaster as far as sex was concerned. There was a lot of uneasy fumbling and panting. I kept looking up expecting to find a bunch of giggling brats spying on us. I kissed Rose with such amateur passion that her lower lip turned swollen and purple. Then I lost the condom in the ferns. When it eventually turned up – covered in grime and grass – the romance simply slid away.

Rose and I broke up the next day. She told her mother she'd burst her lip in a fall.

In August, the Big Blokes entered a team for a new northside soccer tournament. Nessan and I were invited to join, mainly because they were short of players. I knew they must have been particularly hard up because Big John himself asked me to join.

The Big Match was played at Howth Celtic's ground in the town. There was a large crowd and goalposts and nets and special strips for the team. It was just like the real thing. I played at right full-back. Nessan was in goal.

For twenty minutes we were magnificent. I made adventurous runs from the back and delivered the pass for our first goal. Nessan made several daring, spectacular saves.

Then someone accidently kicked Nessan on the face during a goalmouth melee, I had to hoof the ball over my own crossbar to prevent the other team scoring in the confusion.

Nessan was taken off to the doctor. Big John insisted that I take Nessan's place in goal. I protested, but everyone overruled me.

The first shot I had to face was a timid effort from forty yards. It trickled past me into the net. The next effort hit me in the knees, bounced twice, and rolled in. Everything that came my way went into the net. At half-time, we were losing by fifteen goals to one. Even the referee stopped counting. That was the end of my career as a Big Bloke.

It was also my last full summer in Howth. After that I went to college, moved around, started work, did the usual things. I seldom went back.

Six years ago, my parents sold their house and moved first to Galway, then Rathmines. I fell out of touch with my old hometown, and most of my old pals.

Now, I live in Dalkey, on the opposite side of the bay. My old home is directly across the water. Most days, I can just make out the pale stub of the Bailey lighthouse.

Occasionally, a morning mist covers all the familiar landmarks on the top of the hill and leaves me feeling like a "runner", with no real knowledge or feeling for Howth at all. On such mornings, I feel as though I never knew the place — merely caught a glimpse of it while passing through.

DEAD BONES AND CHICKENS
Roddy Doyle

A new path has been laid at one end of the green in Kilbarrack. There are other paths missing and there's a scabby old field beside the tracks doing nothing, but when I saw this new path a month ago the thought hit me – it's finished. They've finished building Kilbarrack.

I can now get to the Giant shopping centre without getting muck on my trousers. It's a pity it's closed down.

The green is a great place. It has a weather system all of its own. The rain doesn't fall on the green. It gallops across it. It waits for you. It surrounds you like the Apaches, jabs at you and wriggles in under your coat. It breaks the nose off you. Even on a dry day you can get drenched crossing the green.

On summer evenings the green is full of people. Thin kids in tracksuits run round and around it and stockier kids run quicker across it. There are Golfing Prohibited signs and the golfers lean against them while they wait for the lads in front to finish. Sometimes there are horses. Polo isn't prohibited. And there is soccer, what looks like three matches being played on the one pitch at the same time. The fathers stand on the sideline and shout, Good lad Darren and Mind your house. The kids all run after the ball.

Last September there was a dead body on the green for a couple of hours. R.T.E. came out. The next Saturday there was another dead body there.

Ah Jaysis, not another one!

But he was only drunk. The guards took him home.

At Halloween there are bonfires on the green; cardboard boxes, wooden pallets from the supermarkets, bags of rubbish, sometimes a tyre and, once, the clinic. The day after that one the road was covered in nappies and files.

Yesterday my first year Group Cert class recited the Great Deserts of the World for me.

Sahara, Kalahari, Gobi, Dollymount. Sahara, Kalahari, Gobi, Dollymount.

They burst out laughing everytime they got to Dollymount.

The church in Kilbarrack is one of those pyramid jobs, with a tape of a bell instead of a real one. The old church is now the snooker hall. The old church isn't very old. I was delighted when it was built. It meant that I could now go to mass on my own and, later, pretend to go to mass on my own. Before that we had to go to Baldoyle for mass, the whole family. By the time my parents got their act together there was usually only the half-twelve mass left, and we weren't allowed out because we were in our good clothes. We drove to Baldoyle. My father pointed up to a window in the convent there and told us that that was where they kept the black babies. Sometimes the half-twelve mass was a Requiem mass and it went on forever. I sat there, squashed and sweating, hoping that someone would faint, especially an altar boy, especially the one holding the bell. Kilbarrack's own church was a great escape. I'll never play snooker in it.

Last week I met a past pupil at Kilbarrack station. He's twenty two. He left the army last year.

They made us get up before the fuckin' seagulls, Mister Doyle.

He's back home now. They call the house Vietnam because they never cut the grass

From our house on Kilbarrack Road, Howth Junction seemed like miles away. But then they widened and straightened the road and chopped down the hedges and there it was, the station, just down there. They dug up the road and put down pipes. Then they dug it up again and put down more pipes. Houses were replacing the cows, first private ones and then the corporation ones. Young ones and young fellas took over the paths. I'd heard the word Fuck for the first time in Ballybunion in August 1966. I heard it a lot now. I heard off a lot as well. They put down more pipes. Then the grocer's was sold and became the chipper, and that was it. Kilbarrack had become a new place.

The third years had their town plans on the desks. We were doing street names.

Cooper's Lane?, I asked.

A man that makes barrels lived down there.

Good man. Pearse Street?

Padraic Pearse, said Debbie.

Good. Who was he?

He won the Eurovision Song Contest.

I looked at her. She was grinning.

Mick King was one of the new people. One of us would say – Here's Mick King, and we'd be legging it down Kilbarrack Road or up Kilbarrack Road, anywhere to get away from him. Before Mick King the wildest man in Kilbarrack was the one who'd pissed in the letterbox of one of the shops. And there were the older boys who'd put aspirin in a bottle of coke and got sick over each other and passed out in the fields where Bayside was being built. But Mick King was – Mick King. There were dozens of stories. Mick King broke all the windows in the school, Mick King threw roof slates down at the guards, Mick King skulled a man with a hammer, Mick King set his ma on fire, Mick King hijacked Mister Whippy. I believed all of them. I knew all about Mick King but I don't think I ever saw him.

The day after Hector Grey's warehouse burned down I watched a child emptying his schoolbag. He took out a biro, half a pencil and twenty seven fancy pencil parers. He lined them up at the top of his desk; Papa Smurf, Paddington Bear, Metal Micky, Darth Vader, Zebedee. He let the girl beside him sharpen her pencil with Dougal's arse.

There's still a farmyard in Kilbarrack, on the corner of Kilbarrack Road and Thornville. There are chickens in there, and a smell. I've been told that if you hang around long enough on a Saturday night you'll see all the mammies climbing up over the wall for the Sunday dinner.

Last October I saw Christy on the corridor just outside my

room. He was holding a magnifying glass to the crotch of his trousers and everytime a girl walked past him he made it go bigger, smaller, bigger, smaller.

I roared at him.

Christy! Stop that.

He grinned.

Ah now, Sir, he said. They'll have to learn about it sooner or later.

I'm glad I come from the same place as Christy.

MAIN STREET – NO BRAKES
Raheny
Sara Berkeley

Main Street in Raheny is the most dramatic part of the village. It's on a hill, quite a steep hill when you're freewheeling down on someone's backer and they're shouting that the brakes won't work. The zebra crossing at the end is where the odd guy's house was. There's always a man in a village whom the kids are scared of – someone of sufficient mystery for them to invent terrible stories about. The man had an alsatian and he was always building his house. For the whole time I was a kid, this guy was building extensions and attic rooms, glazing, plastering, sawing, while his dog menaced the kids who tried to steal the cement sand. Then he finished his house and I grew up. I left school. I went to college and got a headful of the city. Raheny seemed like a distant suburb.

In fact, Raheny features large on all the roadsigns coming north out of the city.

"What's so great about Raheny?" a south-side friend of mine grumbled once as we drove down the Howth Road at Clontarf. "You'd think it was the only outpost before Howth."

I was tempted to ask him could he list the others, but I kept my counsel. I could have told him that Raheny's part of Europe now – it has a bottle bank! It's down the back of the shopping-centre, beside the river that the Scouts clean once a year. Every troop in Ireland could clean that river once a year and there'd still be SuperValu bags in the bushes; but then it runs under the Howth Road, and when it comes out the other side, it runs by the Scout Den. It gets a bit of a shock there – the 73rds have landscaped the bank with log tiers and shrubs and a bench. The river takes a look at this and runs on

29

ashamed towards Main Street and Manor House.

On the other side from SuperValu is the church carpark, about the size of Mayo, but nicely scaled to the airport-hangar of Raheny Church. I know the carpark intimately. I used to study it glumly on Sundays from the porch steps, while the blood slowly returned to my head. I was always getting dizzy at mass when I was a kid and with a church that size you had to sit near a door or you'd never make it. It was built before I was born but it's still called the New Church. The old church is a youth club, when it's not burned down.

Raheny is a huge sprawling place and I'm not clear where the boundaries are. Over the years bits got lopped off – Grange, Edenmore. Down the end of my road is Kilbarrack. Foxfield's across The Field. They blocked up the lane that linked Foxfield with St. Assams. There were "undesirable gangs" hanging round. It was a great lane and I had a lot of fun being in an undesirable gang there when I was a kid. The Field is a marsh, but we thought of it as a swamp. If you strayed off the path...well...a shoe had been found...a glove.

The Field stretched the length of St.Assams and all the houses on Foxfield Road backed on to it. At the edge was a great ditch. I kissed a boy there when I was 9. He was having his 13th birthday and we celebrated his entrance into adulthood maturely, sitting on the wall outside McGreevy's newsagent drinking red lemonade. Down in The Field he told me and my friend about frenchies and The Five Stars. I've never heard of The Five Stars since. We smoked cigarettes – I was quite a rebel for a short time. Another great place for kissing boys was behind the library. Once a man exposed himself there, but the boy I was with wouldn't let me look. Then I went to the convent for six years and forgot everything useful I had learned. The worst I got up to there was sticking my head in the door of the dry-cleaner's, going home on winter days. The warmth was great and I'd been told the smell of the cleaning agent could get you high. The dry-cleaning lady didn't seem very happy in spite of breathing it in all day. She was always shouting "SHUT THE DOOR!"

Raheny has quite a history: there's St. Anne's for example, the park that used to be the grounds for a grand old Guinness house; and the lovely Protestant church attached, which both my grannies attended. When you're in the grounds it's hard to believe you're still in the 20th century. My father told me how the great trees along the Howth Road there used to flank the drive from the house down to the church. I had visions of elegant carriages and Raheny as it might have been then, with the Old Church, the Crescent (a semicircle of ancient stone cottages opposite the airport-hangar) and Main Street, long long long before bicycles were ever thought of.

RAHENY
Hilary Fannin

My first journey was from the Leinster nursing home on Leeson street to St. Assams Avenue Raheny. A Christian suburb, a parish, a village. There were houses on our road that bore more houses, and Chapelizod was exotic enough to be on the other side of the world.

There were children on my road with mothers. I had a plaster virgin with a golden crown. My granny once brought home a plastic virgin with a blue crown, but she leaked her holy water blood on the floor.

Next door's mother had seven girls. My mother said they'd be Ban Gardas. My mother had a fun fur coat and took lifts in a red Hillman Hunter.

There were two schools in our parish. The National school had girls who walked to school in tartan skirts, to teachers with big sticks and maps, who beat them, said my father in the car.

And my school with the nuns. In May we walked around the tennis court clutching beads, and prayed to the spring time virgin who minded the dead babies in limbo, until our chants released them. I thought I saw them in the sky, spinning in my mother's blue washing basket, waiting to take flight like starlings.

There was a chapel in our school with wooden pews and old nuns. I made my first communion there, with gold stars on the roof, and afterwards a breakfast in the lunch room, with butter shaped like golf balls and an ice cream to bring home. I walked gently to my waiting father, so full of sanctifying grace I thought I'd spill.

There were corridors in our school, very shiny, with tiles in blue and black and white. Going home at three o'clock our outdoor shoes were for the black tiles. By day our indoor shoes tread the blue tiles. And as a special treat our ballet shoes and plimsoles were allowed to walk on the white tiles. There was a fine of sixpence for each transgression and a lifetime fear of putting your foot wrong.

I was lonely on my road and sensed the National childrens' fear and disapproval. At school I learnt of purgatory and little crosses, I looked into my life for things to bear. My mother dyed her hair blonde, joined a band and started singing.

I ran fast down our road and drew the curtains. I thought the darkness could protect her, from neighbouring faces smelling around our door.

I practised walking down our road with my eyes closed but felt each household's new extensions, their venetian blinds and double door intrusions.

My mother went to London, came home again and brought me a purple polo neck with a golden buckle. I celebrated running down our road with my poncho gathered around my waist, regal bad and getting louder. My sister threw a stone through her bedroom window and in defiance outlined the crack with scarlet nail polish.

When the bailiffs came I smelt our neighbours on their knees, offering up their crosses, offering up their leftovers to their God, who must protect them from the politics of their estate. They knew then a house empty of a polished proclamation could drift into a pagan isolation.

I feared them, their road, their mantillas, their cousins in Leitrim, their hymns and confirmation suits.

The bailiffs took the piano, chairs and tables. The bank reclaimed their urban patch, and the nuns dissolved into their wooden nooks and crannies, handing back my books and shoe bag as they withdrew.

We left. Then it was Saturday.

DECKCHAIRS IN DARNDALE
Aileen O'Meara

Finally, they're doing up Darndale. Dublin Corporation, after 14 years, are spending over 10m million, turning the back doors to the front, putting in fireplaces, giving people gardens and front porches. After years of campaigning, the Corporation finally listened to the local people who live in what became a disastrous experiment in community architecture.

Finished in 1976, Darndale, the 950 houses in the estate on the fringes of north Dublin city, was meant to be a form of inner-city type community living in a suburb. "A low-rise, low-cost, high density housing conurbation" was how architects Lardner and Partners described it. Another description was "condensed suburbia". The neighbours called it "Legoland".

Within a few years, it became, through official neglect, bureaucracy, lack of resources and a serious lack of social planning, a ghetto on the edge of the north city. "It is a warren of little alleyways, courtyards and squares", said local Workers Party TD, Pat McCartan.

"I remember when they were building it, at the beginning it was welcomed because it was low-rise and people thought it was clever. But it was a dark colour, the site work was very poorly completed, and the services that were meant to be put there never materialised. There was a view that the drainage was never properly put in at all."

When residents wanted to grow a few flowers in the inches of space at the front of their houses, they were told that it would interfere with "cleaning underground pipes". They named the five parts of Darndale that met in the centre after four flowers: Tulip Court, Primrose Grove, Snowdrop Walk, Buttercup Park and Marigold Court.

And because of the failure to construct soft landscaping and give permission for tenants to grow their own small gardens, the place became a "sea of concrete", the opposite of what was intended. As one local wag put it, "the only flowers in Darndale are the Four Flowers."

Built around the concept of communal grouping of houses around courtyards and safe areas, Darndale has become so unsafe in the minds of many people that doctors are escorted there at night, ambulances have been stolen while the drivers went looking for their sick, bus drivers have refused to drive beyond the roundabout, shopkeepers could not be convinced to open for business. Taxis won't go in there at night sometimes.

Low rise was important in 1973 when it was begun. It was six years after the grandiose plans for the high-rise Ballymun had gone awry as serious social problems grew on the periphery of Glasnevin.

There was a reaction against high rise as an answer to the housing shortages caused by the decanting of the city's inner city communities. Interestingly, half of the original Darndale tenants came from Ballymun; most of them were happy to move there.

Its origins were in a scheme built in Andover, in Kent in England, the concept of an "expanding town" in neighbourhood units which had won an architectural award the year before

Darndale was conceived.

The late Sixties saw the Radburn planning principles in vogue, the creation of neighbourhood units, with major distributor roads encircling them. The units in turn would have their own internal system of traffic and minor and local roads, separating traffic from pedestrians.

In reality, local TDs and visitors still get lost trying to get around the place. They call it a warren. The "kids" used the link road for joyriding.

Experts said of the Radburn planning principle at the time: "The overall impression when walking through the estate

(Andover in Hampshire in England) is that of a civilised order which generates a corresponding sense of responsibility among its occupants. The social impact of this architectural setting of the scene, could be observed when some tenants spontaneously brought their deckchairs out and gathered in a sunny corner, sheltered from the wind, for a friendly chat while their young children were playing happily under their eyes."

Deckchairs in Darndale?

The architects, Lardners, had felt that this design would avoid the "usual characteristics of new estates": "a vast sense of emptiness, producing a sea of concrete; a lack of sense of identity and scale; low standard of safety for children; excessive distances to be travelled by housewives, and the monotony and lack of interest in the aesthetics and standard of detail in the construction."

Between the courtyards were narrow pedestrian alleyways, with "bridge bedrooms" overhead, bridge-like second storey extensions that connected the facing rows of houses.

The houses were very close together; the theory was that it would do away with the drabness of ordinary estates, and induce community spirit.

What it created was a sense of claustrophobia and depression that is almost unique to the area, and is cited by almost everyone who works and lives there.

The fronts of the houses faced onto quite narrow pedestrian walkways, made dark by the colour of the brickwork, and the low-level bridge bedrooms. Some of the pedestrian malls were only nine feet wide.

The Fire Brigade had difficulty getting in. The doctor's car was stolen at night.

At the back of the houses were so-called "gardens", finished with cheap hoarding, onto largely unused space at the back, which rapidly became dirty and full of litter.

Because the fronts of the houses faced inwards, the first view of the estate to the person travelling in from the outside is the ugly and unkempt hoardings and litterstrewn open spaces, devoid of any form of diverting trees, landscaping, or beauty.

It is ugly, depressing and awful.

On the green space at the back, flocks of white seagulls feed off the detritus of litter and the muck from the nearby factories. Darndale was cut off for a long time from its Coolock hinterland by the industrial estate.

Rubbish collection was already made difficult by the fact that bins had to be brought to the end of the malls to be collected, leading to dragging and extensive littering of walkways. What made it worse was that the county council, who had the responsibility to collect the rubbish, did so the day AFTER Dublin Corporation cleaned it. Eventually, this was sorted out.

The appearance of the place, already deteriorating with the bad quality of brickwork and fittings, was made worse by the poorly built pathways and common areas. There was widespread seepage on the pathways, especially in the courtyards and play areas, and flooding and drainage became a particular problem.

Bad maintenance and high litter rates were made worse in an estate with a claustrophobic and intense layout like Darndale.

"In other estates, with similar defects, this fact might not be so important, but in Darndale, where these malls and courtyards constitute the semi-private areas, and communal living space, its depressing effects are probably greater than usual," said Declan Redmond, a student in TCD's Dept of Geography, who studied Darndale.

There were severe problems with the sewerage system, and the drainage and electricity and other developmental works were laid out in a complexity that defied explanation.

Heating problems - only Tulip Court had chimneys on the houses; the rest built in the flush of pre-oil crisis optimism about central heating. The "bridge bedrooms" were badly ventilated, and cold and difficult to heat. Some had structural faults, and needed to be reinforced. Damp was a problem.

Residents surveyed about their views about landscaping and improving the area, said they were very interested in setting plants and shrubs in the areas provided in the plan. But the areas around the courtyards, which were originally intended for planting, were filled in with concrete. There were play areas assigned for children; but few facilities were made available. "The kids" became responsible for a lot of the widespread graffiti and vandalism around Darndale.

Between 1973 and 1976, most of Darndale was completed. They were built cheaply, to the "low cost" requirement laid down by the Corporation. In the long run, the Corporation paid dearly for its mistake. The estate cost over 4.5m to complete in 1976; last year, the first two phases of the refurbishment plan cost 2.2m, and there are another six phases to go.

People were moved in, but the planned high level of community facilities did not materialise. When the estate was built, a school and parochial hall were constructed. Four years later, the only additions for the four and a half thousand population were two small inadequate shops, a grocer and a newsagent. The estate's reputation led to a strong reluctance by shopkeepers to open shops. People had a 25-minute walk to the Northside Shopping Centre to get to shops, and the health clinic and to the chemist. They signed on in the city centre.

It was a very young population that initially settled. By 1979, over 4,500 people lived there, the average age of parents was 32, the average age of the eldest child was nine the average age of the youngest was 3.

The highest number of residents was in the 20-45 age group; the second highest was in the 0-5 age group, and there were very few people over 60.

People with low incomes, cut off from their natural hinterland, were placed in a severely deprived environment, with few services, bad public transport, cut off from other housing by a big industrial estate, off the main road, feeling increasingly isolated and ignored.

Crime soared, the place looked awful, and the "address" syndrome for jobs created a vicious circle.

Community spirit up to the mid-eighties was lacking, as factions developed within the estate and people like Linda Brady and her family fell victim to unpopularity.

The 19-year-old teenager believed there were "bad people" there, to use her own words. She was speaking just days after her 19-year-old common law husband had been stabbed in Darndale, leaving her with three children, baby Gerard, Kevin, 2, and Jason 3, over two years ago in one of the many incidents that had made the place notorious. That was in October 1988.

Still coping with the death of the father of her children, the teenage mother then experienced a litany of shocking experiences that in many ways encapsulated the uncontrolled and dangerous nature of the claustrophic complex.

The evening after her husband was stabbed, her house, with all its belongings and memories, was burnt down, leaving her destitute and homeless.

She moved in with her husband's sister, Martina Johnson, also in Darndale.

Days later, a gang of men including some from the north inner city, rampaged and tore apart Martina's home, forcing her onto the street outside with her family and belongings.

A sister of Martina's and the dead man also moved out of her home around the corner. The three women slept in Margaret's husband's car, near their homes, with their eight children scattered amongst neighbours and family.

"They had machetes, and chains, and iron bars, and they threw rocks through the windows," a terrified Margaret Egan said at the time.

The three women moved out of Darndale, nearer to their families in nearby Coolock and Kilbarrack. Linda Brady is now living in nearby Belcamp Lane.

"I would say that point one of one percent of the population are responsible for much of the bad name that Darndale developed," said the local Garda Sergeant. "Most of the people up there are ordinary decent people, working against the odds to do the best for their kids."

"We have two community policemen on foot patrols in the area now, it's a new concept. It's working fairly well. One of the guards was hit on the head with a brick a few months ago

40

but he is now back on the beat."

Most of the Garda calls to Darndale concern family disputes, squatters and car thefts. "It got a bad name because of the way that it looked. It was difficult to police it; the policemen were never consulted before it was built.

Putting a lot of people into a very small area never works."

One of the three Juvenile Liaison Officers for the area is certain that poverty is the chief source of the high level of social problems there, particularly juvenile crime.

"No wonder a child is stealing, a child needs to survive," he said. "It's not a stable environment, there are no trees or flowers, the play areas are terrible. It was a great idea that traffic would not be allowed around the fronts of houses, but it looked terrible after a while."

Another garda there said it was never a "no-go" area, but "you needed to know where you were going" when you went in there.

Low school attendance, and child abuse, is a general problem in the area, "kids of 4 or 5 are as streetwise as 10 to 11 year olds elsewhere. When parents have to work to make ends meet, they leave it to older kids to take care of the younger ones. There's not much supervision."

Within a few years of moving in, people wanted to get out.

By the early 80s, one third of the population was on the transfer list, and there was a low level of sales of houses to tenants; people were reluctant to stay. A NESC survey from that time showed that 60% of people wanted out.

Like many other parts of local authority Dublin coping to create a community spirit against the odds, Darndale lost some of its community leaders in 1984 when the 5,000 surrender grant for local authority tenants to buy their own private houses gave many people the exit they wanted.

A study by Threshold found that over 18% of Darndale tenants, higher than average, applied for the grant, and most of them moved to nearby areas, those with jobs left in large num-bers. And as the number of vacancies arose, the incidence of lettings to single parents with one child and childless couples rose.

"The Corporation helped turn it into a ghetto, by the low quality of its fabric and appearance. They then put people with serious social problems into it, because it was low demand. Single parent families, people evicted from their own houses, people whose marriages had broken up – people who were singularly incapable of managing for themselves, people who needed special attention," said Pat McCartan.

In 1987, of the 210 lettings of houses in Darndale, (one fifth of the estate), 119 went to single parent families.

When the free beef was distributed frozen in 1986, courtesy of the EC Food mountains, the dank smell of poverty and dirt was temporarily replaced in the narrow malls by the mouthwatering smell of sides of quality beef, something many people in the estate rarely ate.

The then EC Combat Poverty Project there found in 1985 that they had to instruct people how to cook it, so unusual was it for people to have large cuts of defrosting meat.

"People don't buy roasts and large cuts of beef here, " said a community worker. "We had to tell people how long to cook it for. And a lot of people did not realize that you can't freeze the meat twice."

Unemployment is running at nearly 50% of the population.

"The only professionals in Darndale are the ones who come into the estate every day and leave it every evening," said one worker. "There's a huge input of social services, from the ISPCC to the youth services."

Despite all the setbacks, things are now improving.

As a result of the successful refurbishment plan (the result of pressure from tenants) which is landscaping the common areas, turning the entrances around to the front, with enclosed front gardens, and replacing the dark modular look with dashing, things are looking up.

The new image means there are now no vacant houses, and there is a waiting list of 80 families waiting to move in.

The Corporation has appointed a full time housing officer for the estate, responsible for transfer arrangements, for repairs and maintenance, with an office in the estate.

Maybe the deckchairs will be out this summer.

COOLOCK
Paul Kimmage

My brother was in Coolock the day Ireland beat England in the European soccer championships. He was in a pub, having a wee in the wake of the celebrations, when a stranger in his mid forties joined him in front of the porcelain. "Do you know", said the man, "this is the happiest day of my life."

My brother told me of his meeting later and I was shocked. How sad for a televised game of football to represent a man's most memorable day in life. And how pathetic. I have thought of him often when driving through Coolock's streets, streets that shaped him, gave him nothing. I've tried so many times to put a face on him. But so many faces seem to fit. He is Coolock.

My parents moved to Kilmore Avenue, half way between Northside Shopping Centre and Artane Castle, when I was six. At the time the shopping centre was just a green field on the other side of the Oscar Traynor road and the castle, part of the huge estate of the St. David's Christian Brothers where I went to school.

I remember the excitement when the shopping centre opened. They built a swimming pool on the roof and as we queued I would imagine the walls suddenly cracking and the water gushing down through the ceiling of the Five Star supermarket and making all the cornflakes soggy.

Coolock was fun in my pre-teenage years. "Davids" with its farm, playing fields, swimming pool and Norman Wisdom films in the old church on Fridays, was a great school. There were no facilities, nothing was organised but we were at an age when it didn't seem to matter.

A trip through the narrow bushes to the old iron boat at the top of Skelly's lane was the ultimate adventure. We used the wide open spaces to the maximum. We'd play "Tarzan" on the trees and there was football and stone-throwing and bee-catching — the skill of crouching down with a jam jar with a perforated lid and coaxing a red arse off a buttercup without him stinging you. Or trying to make frogs out of tadpoles we'd fish from streams, or jumping over yard brushes and bits of building materials when Eddie Macken was on the telly.

So when did it all change? When did Coolock acquire its "reputation", become one of the most expensive areas in Dublin to insure a home?

I remember me Ma sending me to the butcher to buy meat for the dinner one day. I went on my bike and it was robbed. I couldn't believe it, walking out of the butcher's with the pork chops in my hand and seeing nothing. I cried all the way home, it broke my heart.

This was my first lesson.

The green spaces began to disappear during my teenage years, housing estate after housing estate in the spaces we used for play. "Davids" was no longer such a fun place either — the farm had closed up, much of the playing fields were sold for development, and there was study and exams and pressure.

Ma made me write Artane as our address when I was applying for jobs. She had this thing about employers reading "Coolock" at the bottom of the application and instantly throwing it in the bin. Perhaps she was right, Coolock received a lot of bad press at the time between joyriding and the 27B bus drivers getting mugged and young men swinging from the neck on trees they had once played "Tarzan" on.

I was lucky, my parents kept a tight rein on me during those difficult development years. I was guided, encouraged, assisted. I got a job and have done okay. I suppose I'm a bit of a snob now. I sip wine, prefer my steak *au point* (medium), drink my coffee black (only percolated), appreciate Pavarotti (admittedly only since the World Cup), work south of the Liffey, mix in the best circles and live in a nice house in the country. I have arrived.

So where is Coolock?

It's a suburb without an identity. A place to watch televised football and live the happiest days of your life.

BURIED MEMORIES
June Considine

The rivers have been buried under glass domed shopping
centres. They run silent now, neatly channelled under rows of
suburban houses. A stream lined dual carriageway, hot with
the pulse of traffic, cuts a swathe through the memories of my
childhood. All my life I have lived close to water. I was born
under the sign of Cancer and, true to my birth sign, spent the
first four years of my life within sight and sound of the Grand
Canal. One day my mother began painting pictures with
words. She saw beyond the high ceilinged flat where we lived
in Herbert Place, past the hum of city life to a quiet, rural
village called Finglas.

They were magic words. A long back garden all to myself. A
front door which would only be used by my family. Outside
the windows of our flat I could hear the deep throb of barges
going by with their cargo of turf and flour. I wondered if the
canal would flow past our new home? "No," said my mother.
"But there will be rivers, clear and free flowing, everywhere
you look."

But it was the canal which filled the wonder of my
imagination. One evening, before we moved, I climbed out
onto our third floor window sill. I waved and crawled closer to
the edge as a magnificent white barge chugged by. The world
beneath me paused and grew very still, only breathing again as
my mother's strong arms encircled me and drew me back
inside. No doubt as she packed our belongings she breathed a
prayer of thanksgiving that we were moving to the security of
the countryside.

It was 1949 and Finglas was the countryside. Finglas Park,
our new home, smelled of dust, cement and fresh paint.

It was part of a similar network of roads and avenues,

initially built for members of the Church of Ireland congregation. It was an ambitious project which failed because there was an insufficient number of the faithful willing to move to such an isolated setting. When the houses went on the open market they were bought by Catholics, mainly with a rural background.

They took their roots with them. Neighbouring roosters greeted the dawn and many gardens contained rambling chicken runs with sods of turf, dug from the bog allotments on the Wicklow mountains, stacked against the garden walls. Every house had a high saddled bicycle in the hall. It was the only means of transport in those days and most men, no matter how great the distance, thought nothing of cycling to work.

My memories of those early days are fragmented, condensed into Sunday afternoon strolls with my parents and Deirdre, my sister who had been born three months after our move, sitting like a queen in her pram as I wheeled it down Ballygall Road. We would walk past Craigies land with its herd of grazing cattle while my mother gathered bunches of overhanging hawthorn blossom. The leaves cast filagrees of sun shadows before us and each rocky wall seemed to have a river trickling quietly behind it. They shimmered in the heart of every gully.

Yet even in those days the rivers of Finglas were fighting a losing battle. Sometime after we settled into our new home an underground tributary which had been buried beneath our estate, defied its concrete grave and surfaced in a neighbour's dining room. The excitement on the street was intense as its short lived resurrection seeped through the new furnishings and fittings. Then it was grimly channelled back beneath the foundations of our lives. But other rivers ran free and unhindered by the new estates which were beginning to fan out on either side of the village. The devil lurked beneath the arches of An Fionn Glas which weaved through the centre of Finglas. No one knew how the story originated. If it matured in the folk lore of Old Finglas or was born in the rich imagination of a new generation of school children. The nuns could preach all they liked about fires of damnation but we knew better.

The river lay in the shade of the old grave yard on Wellmount Road where, and this was another irrefutable fact, a body had once been buried alive. There were two ways of going to our red bricked school on top of Church Street and each had its own avenue of fear through which we must thread. As we rounded the corner of Montgomery's, the butchers, and neared the bridge of An Fionn Glas we would hear the roar of water. It would tease our fears and beckon us over clumps of nettles and scutch grass until we stood on the edge of the river bank. "Can you see the devil," we would challenge each other and tremble as we saw him wavering beneath the tangled reeds and slime covered stones.

If we decided to avoid the devil and travel the Church Street route we would meet The Man. He lived in one of a row of small cottages near the school. Tall and white haired with a bushy moustache, he would stand, stooped in his doorway and suddenly begin shouting, in a shell shocked voice, rambling memories, triggered off on the killing fields of Europe. "A war victim," our mothers said, touching their fingers to their heads. "He was shell shocked during the war." We accepted him just as we accepted our disappearing countryside, the rows of houses which now widened the narrow lanes and the new children, with their thin city faces, who filled the classrooms to overflowing.

The small cottages and bungalows of Old Finglas looked tired. Like old people dispossessed of a past as they crouched on the edge of the new estates. There was an energy in the air as more and more families arrived from all over Dublin to shape the future of Finglas. Schools and shops were being built, yet, for a long time, the village remained untouched.

The Blanchardstown Mills served flour, oatmeal and sugar from sacks. Farmers bought meal for their cattle. Wide sides of bacon hung from hooks in the ceiling and butter was cut from a golden block and shaped between two wooden paddles.

There was a corner shop beside the post office. I think it was called Fagans and I remember one old woman selling penny ice creams and sweets wrapped in a cone of newspaper. The post office was an institution, dust beams trapped in the sunlight as it slanted through the narrow doors. The smell of gum and wax. Miss Luby, the post mistress, grim and grey haired, an acid tongue which she used on adult and child alike.

Herds of cattle meandered through the main street. "They're going to the slaughter house," we'd shout and, torn between pity and curiosity, would follow them down through the village and watch as they disappeared through the high gates of Montgomerys.

Milk was delivered by Mr. Lawlor who stood tall and steady on his milk float. It was pulled by a pony and he poured out pints of milk from a long handled silver jug. The Merville Dairy men were more sophisticated with their horse drawn carts and crates of bottled milk. On a hot day we always seemed to have a visit from the malodorous "slops carts" and the women would come out with their bins of potatoe peelings and left-over vegetables which would be used as pig food. Farming life was still a visible part of Finglas.

Yet everywhere we looked we could see deep rivulets of development. Foundation trenches filled with muddy water. The rainbow sheen of petrol printing patterns on embedded tyre tracks. Although we did not understand what was happening we must have instinctively understood that an old way of life was changing forever when we trespassed, late one evening, on a building site where Ballymun Avenue, later to be known as Glasnevin Avenue, was being built. We carried a tin box filled with secret diaries and other bric-a-brac of childhood which we buried beneath the heavy mud.

As the fields gave way to concrete we discovered Finglas Woods. It was a wild place, full of unexplored undergrowths and mysterious passageways leading through the trees. We learned to swing from the low branches like monkeys. We would sway back and forth with the sun warm on our upside down faces. But, as always, it was the river which attracted as it ran through the centre of the woods.

Shoes were immediately discarded as soon as we arrived and we would spend meticulous hours building dams from rocks and broken branches as we re-routed its course. It was a floating playground, jealously guarded and if a rival gang tried to invade our stretch of water, we kicked and scratched our way to victory.

At the edge of the woods a large pipe, possibly a sewage tunnel, spanned a deep ravine. The river flowed far below, banked by spires of crusted clay and rocks. If we wished to reach the far side of the woods where a grassy slope spilled down to the river, we would skip across the stepping stones. More often, however, as we tried to slip quietly out of our houses, we were waylaid by determined mothers who would insist on the youngest offspring accompanying us. Then, complete with prams and go-cars, we used the pipe. While our mothers enjoyed a brief respite from their responsibilities little did they realise that their babies were sitting snugly in their deep bellied prams, calmly sucking their soothers as we walked across the pipe, never once looking down in case we lost concentration, wheels balanced precisely on the sloping sides.

The years passed quickly, scattering the seeds of image and memory. The Spanish nuns came to a new convent beside the woods and taught us embroidery in soft, broken English accents. On summer evenings we explored the undergrowth of their gardens and a crushed garlic smell would rise from the delicate white flowers beneath our feet. We had ballet lessons in the high old house which sat like a brooding doyen over the Bottom of the Hill pub. Concerts and Ceilis were held in the Parochial hall. It was the only centre for entertainment in the village and my most abiding memory is of an old white haired man, Mr O'Brion, with his green beret tilted to the side of his head as he talked to us in Irish and roused our young hearts to a frenzy of republican fervour.

On the 17th. of March the religious processions began. We would gather at St. Canice's Church and wend our way towards St. Patrick's well which was surrounded by swamps and history. The May procession was heavy with the scent of lilac and girls in white Communion dresses. Corpus Christi left us all in a state of exhaustion. It decked the streets in bunting and the swell of voices as we sang our way through endless estates with red sashed stewards ordering us onward, Children of Mary cloaks flapping around our ankles and the sun, beating down from the merciless blue sky.

We took our religion for granted. Sunday night benediction and the Monday Night novenas were packed out with young people who, either mutinously or obediently, attended these rituals every week. But it was the religion of the Protestant children who lived around us which we found fascinating. We sensed a more privileged background. Smaller families were the norm and the girls all seemed to have peachy skin and a straight shouldered walk. They could join mysterious organisations called the Girl Guides and went camping in brown uniforms with strange badges and emblems. We could console ourselves all we liked that we, alone, held the key to the kingdom of heaven. But it was a poor swop.

They too were curious about our religion and often we would gather at each other's gates to discuss what it was that set us apart each Sunday.

We held masses in our back gardens, a milk crate serving as an altar, a squeaking rubber mouse announcing the consecration. We taught them to genuflect and learned to recite their Our Father.

We were absolutely horrified when one girl, on inspecting her family bible informed us that Jesus had a couple of brothers and there might even be a sister tucked somewhere into his genealogical tree.

Occasionally we would descend from the lofty tones of theology to chant "Proddy Proddy – go to hell. Ringing out the Devil's bell" and the answer would automatically follow "Catty Catty – go to mass. Riding on the Devil's ass."

As our religion strictly refused us entry to a Protestant place of worship the tree shaded old church on the borders of Finglas West drew us like a magnet. We would stand outside the wrought iron gates and read the wooden notice giving details of the weekly service as we tried to work up the courage to venture inside. But having been assured that such acts of heresy were prone to punishment by direct bolts of lightning we never dared. And the mystery grew.

Despite my parent's rural background I grew up in an extended family. Around the corner on Clune Road lived my Uncle Eoin and Aunt Brigid. They had three sons and, early on in life, I decided to marry the middle one, Gerry. He refused, point blank, to accept my proposal and once, in an act of desperation, drank a pint of holy water to prove his determination to be a priest. For both of us life wended in different ways as it did for my Aunt Rosaleen and Uncle Paddy who lived next door to us and later emigrated to England.

My Aunt Rosaleen and my mother were sisters and the children who were born to them both in the following years were all around the same age.

Nurse Flaherty, the midwife, was a busy woman. Hospital births were a rarity and most babies were born in front of blazing bedroom fires while we watched steaming delph basins of water disappearing behind closed doors. Some time later we would hear the thin kittenish cry and a new baby brother would be introduced to us. First came my brother Roger whose nerve would later be tempered on the pipe walk across Finglas Woods. Four years later my brother Dermot was born.

On that night I lay in bed with my sister and listened to the sounds from next door in my parent's bedroom. They were removed from the everyday sounds, a muffled cry, the patient voice of Nurse Flaherty, footsteps on the stairs, the strained face of my Aunt Rosaleen as she came in and asked us to stay very quiet. Later, when Nurse Flaherty had uncoiled the umbilical cord from around my brother's throat and he began to cry from thin, blue lips, a silence settled, like a prayer over the house.

In the fifties the emigration trail took its toll on Finglas. Three families moved from our block of houses. Among them was my Aunt and, for a long time afterwards, it felt as if part of our lives had been amputated. Family partings were a feature of our childhood. My father worked for a shipping line and I remember my parent's life together as one of long absences remember my parent's life together as one of long absences and brief, emotional homecomings.

On the day of his arrival home we would meet him as he stepped from the 35 bus and bear him, like a prized possession, home to my mother. Rogie and Bridie – they had so little time to spend their love together and for the next few days we would tip toe around their absorption with each other. From being the pivot of our mother's life we would suddenly find ourselves in its background as they hugged each other in discreet corners and threw besotted looks at each other across the dining room table. We accepted it all with good grace and knew that she would return to normal within a few days of his leaving. We never understood or appreciated her loneliness and she never imposed it on us.

When he left again we would stand at the door and wait until he rounded the corner of Clune Road. He would always pause, look back and lift his hand in a gesture of farewell. We would wave madly in return until he was out of sight before beginning the long wait for his return. My mother would then settle down to writing long detailed letters to him. She would chart the daily routine of the family and bring it to life for him in distant ports around the world.

One afternoon, when my Aunt Rosaleen still lived next door to us, she called into my mother for a chat. *The Evening Press* had been delivered and lay on the table, unread, between them. As she spoke my mother casually glanced at a headline. The words danced before her eyes and she cried out in a breathless voice.

CAMEO IN DANGER OF SINKING read the headline. It was the ship on which my father worked.

It had gone aground on a sandbank along the Wexford Coast and, claimed the news report, if the evening tide did not refloat her, she would sink. Without a telephone there was nothing my mother could do except wait for the evening news. My aunt sat with her through the long hours until word came through that the crew had been rescued by lifeboat.

When my father arrived home he handed me a rag doll with

a painted china face. As the crew abandoned ship they had left most of their personal possessions behind them. But he had managed to slip the presents he had brought home to us into the back pocket of his trousers. In honour of the occasion we called the doll *Cameo*.

Tragedy also played its part in our young lives. Diptheria came to our estate. I can still see groups of women standing by their gates, silently waiting out the last breath of a young boy who lived up the road from us. Perhaps it was not dark when he died. Maybe it was just the light leaving their faces that I remember as word rippled down the street and, for a few days afterwards, we were treated with a strange fragile gentleness.

Polio also took its toll. Soon we would see the twisted bodies of young boys and girls, some in wheel chairs, some struggling on callipers, thin shoulders hunched with determination. Vaccination became the in word. Processions of children in vests and pants, pimples on our arms, sugar lumps and X ray vans.

When the Casino Cinema came it opened up a whole new world for us. We were not a discerning audience nor had we come under the critical influence of television. The Lone Ranger or Madam X – Tom and Jerry – an exotic Eastern travelogue – even Pathe News was compulsive viewing for nine pennies. We cheered and yelled warnings to the chap, booed the Villain and dodged the usherette with her torch as she tried to order us out after the first showing.

Rock Around the Clock was greeted with hysterical screams and, soon afterwards, the first Teddy Boys began to lurk on the village corners. Drain pipe trousers and long jackets, their hair quiffed with Brylcream into luxurious DAs, they sneered in Jail House Rock fashion as they swaggered past in corrugated rubber soled shoes.

The Casino put its imprimatur on a young couple's relationship if they were seen heading in its direction together for more than two successive Sunday nights. We began to hear stories about the "back row". Strange things happened there. Teenagers giggled and whispered. They threw knowing eyes to heaven when we demanded to know what was so special about the back row. They never told us. It remained another of the great unexplained mysteries until we were old enough to enjoy its anonymous delights.

Suddenly, just as the houses had appeared, young couples were everywhere. They sought the rural privacy of St. Margarets and Dubber Cross and buried themselves deeply in the long grass. They sheltered too in the closed and secret shop doorways and the private back lanes of Sycamore Road. Time was moving on and soon a first generation were planning weddings and a future removed from Finglas.

I married in 1969 and my first step away from Finglas was tentative – to an estate of houses built in Ballygall on Craigie's land. The river, the cattle and Hawthorn blossom had been replaced by neat semi-detached houses. Only the swell of land on which they were built showed the contours of a meadow that once stretched as far as a child's eye could see.

Six months later my mother died. My marriage had marked a maturing of our relationship. We were tentatively reaching towards each others as individuals but it ended on a Sunday afternoon in December. She was buried on the morning before Christmas Eve. As her funeral cortege wended its way through familiar and festive streets people stopped to stare with kindly pity – to cross themselves in a final tribute to her. I felt as if the heart of Finglas had ceased to beat.

Almost twenty years have passed since then. When I return to Finglas I am angered by the destruction of the rural setting. Little was done in its commercial development to hold onto its identity and badly planned shopping centres have imposed an ugliness that was never part of its village streets. Finglas Woods has gone. Initially it was replaced by a sewing factory, built on the crest of grass which sloped to the river. It killed the breath of wind on the trees and today it is the site of a busy shopping centre. Juggernauts flash over the river where we once stood and watched the devil. All that remains is a small shoe repair shop, placed like an incongruous island in the middle of a dual carriageway. It is a monument to obstinance and the rights of a small business to exist in the face of progress.

The Casino has also disappeared. The building still remains but has been absorbed by the Superquinn chain. Banks and fast food, a metal bridge spanning the carriageway, cement boulders blocking entrance to the street where I once walked to school, the trappings of a modern society have reshaped its face. Its pace of life has quickened. It is a pace which is both dynamic and destructive as it responds to the challenges, the problems of an expanding urban town.

Yet my past is caught in the elderly faces that I meet and once knew as the parents of my friends. The houses in East and West Finglas have a settled look. There is a sense of a seasoned community which has known the full span of life and death. Streets where I played are restless with memories. Finglas nurtured my childhood and now it has passed me by. When I return I will always feel that surge of belonging but, although I will never be a stranger to Finglas – it has become a stranger to me.

FACTORY LIFE
Podge Rowan

My most vivid memories of Finglas are centred on the factory; on the people who worked there and the things that happened to them. It was the usual type of building of its era; red-brick front covering the offices and a cantilevered corrugated roof covering the work area. Set in a corner of the sprawling Unidare grounds but not – we were assured – part of Unidare. Especially if there was the threat of a strike.

Our Union was The Irish Transport and General Workers Union or the "Transport" as it was more generally known. Our Union Official would pay a flying visit to the factory in these times of crisis and urge us, plead with us, threaten us if we failed to see his reason – the strike had nothing to do with us!

Nothing to do with us? Just that those picketing the gates were carrying the placards of our own Union! Those on the picket-line were never sure whether they wanted us to support them or not. In the confusion we always passed the picket in the end. What a galling feeling it was to walk by those men sensing their eyes on our backs, and all the assurances about us being one branch and they being another about as helpful as a jar of warm piss.

In the factory itself there were occasional skirmishes between ourselves and the management. The young people in particular were always spoiling for a test of strength. I remember my first strike but what it was about I can't recall. It was hardly a fight really, more of a walkout. But it involved some decision making on my part. As is usual in these affairs one or two people announce their intention of taking action. Others are asked to back them up.

For an hour or so the factory was a ferment of rumours,

whispers and arguments. I remember being urged by an older man to "pay no attention to those trouble makers". Despite this, I joined the walkout, which gained momentum until only a minority were left in the factory.

Looking back it was one of the best decisions I ever made in my life. I think it was from that moment on that I became a rebel. We took on the management and we won. I remember the shame-filled beaten faces of those who had stayed at their work-benches and knew I could never be like them.

I also knew that I never wanted to be a foreman or a chargehand. Their role was particularly unenviable – the meat in the sandwich between the employers and the workers. I remember one man who – against his better judgement – was persuaded to take a supervisor's position and I'm sure that little by little, day after day, it destroyed him.

A factory becomes after a time like an extended family with all the complication of relationships that that implies. Some people found their niche and dug themselves in. Those who left often returned to see how the rest were getting on. If you bumped into one of these "exiles" in the street or a pub you could always expect the sly taunt:

"You still up there? My jeazus – you must have shares in the place by now."

The idea of workers having a greater say in the day to day running of the factory was first raised by our new Shop Steward. This man - a returned emigrant – had a world view. It was a left-wing world view, not at all to the liking of certain sections of management, the Union and a small number of workers.

I can see now that his presence in the role of Shop Steward might have been viewed by those in authority as a challenge. Certainly the ideas he disseminated were a challenge to those of us who supported him. And when the management proposed the introduction of a complicated bonus scheme, the works committee replied with an alternative scheme of their own.

I suppose in the charged atmosphere of that time a strike was inevitable. We didn't win — we couldn't — the ideas were too far ahead of their time. And this was a real strike even without the backing of the Union. This was weeks of walking up and down outside the Unidare gates with workers from the other factories streaming past us. And who could blame them? Hadn't we passed them?

At least we got our own factory entrance out of it. There was no more of one factory passing another factory's pickets. And we went back united, and remained a strong unified work-force for a number of years.

Things change, and our small factory grew its own bunch of unions and inter-union disputes. The bitterness and sometimes the sheer hatred that these disputes provoked left the antagonism between management and worker in the shade. I suppose it's getting back to the family analogy again.

Then came redundancies and there's not much you can do with the spectre of Thatcherism/Monetarism haunting Europe and the world. The fight went out of people and the factory turned in on itself, becoming claustrophobic. I decided it was time to leave. I had another career to pursue.

Since I left the factory has experienced the kind of difficulties that seem to be an ever-present part of the modern business world. I hope it can hang in there and survive. If only to give me the satisfaction of saying (whenever I bump into one of the old mates):

"What — you're still up there? They should have made you a director by now!"

LIVING IN CLAREMONT COURT
Deirdre Purcell

"A housing estate?" I huffed along with my friends when I was young: "I'll never live in a housing estate..."

All of us, me and my friends, came from Pappins Road and Dean Swift Road and other Corpo roads where we lived happily as children. Then some of our parents gained minor promotions at work and we all graduated into the new private housing estates which sprang up around Ballymun. But when we were all teenagers and dreaming together in Drew's Field, we definitely agreed that none of us was going to live in housing estates when we got houses of our own. What we had in mind were character places, period places full of old wood and Agas or cottages surrounded by nothing but fresh air.

Here I am in a housing estate.

Claremont Court, Glasnevin, where I have lived for fifteen years, is within two miles of where I have lived for most of my life and if I ever move again, I suspect it will be within a one-mile radius of here.

When I try to define living here, to distil the experience, I find at first it is inseparable from motherhood. When my sons were very young, the house revolved around them but for them the house was merely an intermission in the state of "out". "Out" was what Claremont Court was all about. "Out" was populated with hordes of other kids and vigilant mothers and fathers; it was littered with skipping ropes and marbles, bikes and skates and prams; "out" ran on the battered wheels of car-pools and Temple Street Hospital was its safety valve.

Later, when even "out" was not enough, I made a deal with my sons. They could join anything they liked, any club or activity, provided they could get themselves there and back safely – and again Claremont Court triumphed. While I got on with my life and work, the boys swam and played basketball and badminton in Vincent's, played tennis in Charleville, learned karate in Phibsboro, ice-skated in the old State cinema, discovered the free videos in the ILAC library, girls in the grounds of Iona Church. Town, just over a mile away, became their local hangout. Had I lived like a lot of my friends in the far suburbs of the south side, I, like them, would have been a slave to the steering wheel.

So much for the boys. They are growing up, almost grown. When they are gone, what will this housing estate mean to me?

If I'm truly honest, not much except in an inverse, Myles na Gopaleen sort of way. I admit I am a northside snob. Quite unfairly, I grit my teeth at the nice little Bennetton girls who play nicely "iteside the hice" on fine days in Sandymount or Stillorgan but I warm to bullet-headed little gurriers who mind cars and groom their ponies on the pitted waste ground less than half a mile from my front door; I desperately want the muesli and mango set who cruise the Merrion and Blackrock centres to come to Superquinn in Finglas and to hear the happy bitching that goes on over the heaps of cabbage. Savagely, I want those who complain about the overcrowded DART to wait twenty-five minutes in the shattered Adshel at the cemetery, while the north wind sweeps down the dual carriageway from Finglas and funeral after funeral turns in at the big iron gates.

I am fiercely proud of the teeming ILAC Centre and love the sports's socks and disposable lighter sellers; I don't need lighters or sports' socks but I buy Kit Kats by the five and velvet hair bands and sets of dangly gilt earrings I will never wear, all the while agreeing with fellow shoppers that the government is a shower of wasters and the price of everything these days is shocking.

To be fair, I tried to live on the southside once. Every weekday for one year I travelled to work as a link in the unbroken chain of cars being winched slowly towards the city centre along by Booterstown and Ballsbridge and

Donnybrook. At weekends, I shopped in shiny tinkling shopping centres and drank plonk in wine bars and agreed it was wonderful at last to be beside the sea.

I was dreadfully unhappy. I fled back to where I belonged. But do I?

Living in a place like this is almost a schizophrenic experience. Claremont Court is not far from some of the most deprived areas in Dublin. Guilt is endemic; why should I have a car, a tree, a house, a job — when up the road, they have nothing to do, little to eat except bread and the cheapest sausages? Who dictated that I should be able to fill my Superquinn basket with fruit and vegetables and real meat, when the trolley in front of me is piled with white sliced pans and tins of Thrift beans? Why should I *not* feel guilty?

On the other hand why should I? Because when it is my aunt who is mugged and dragged behind a motorcycle, my son who is attacked and thrown over a hedge, my car radio ripped off, my tree broken, my house burgled, the quality of tolerance droppeth.

Let's be honest here. I would like to be able to walk along the canal without being stoned or threatened with alsatian dogs; I would like to be able to cross the main road outside the estate using the green light, without danger of being mown down or given the two-finger sign by a trucker in a hurry to Derry. It might be nice to walk to Hart's corner without being choked by diesel fumes or deafened by juggernauts or having to step over streams of old urine from last night's revellers caught short against the broken wall beside the all-weather football pitch.

But let's be more honest here. Claremont Court is a genuinely pleasing place to live — a little island of pleasingness — and thanks to a vigorous Residents' Association, aesthetically good, clean and full of trees and greenery. You can stroll around it looking at its pleasant gardens, chat to pleasant neighbours.

So it's damned if you feel guilty, damned if you don't. It's all to do with confidence in who or what you are. If you get the impression I vacillate wildly in that, I do. I consider carefully the arguments from my left-wing friends who use the word "middle-class" like a whip; I listen equally carefully to the arguments from my right-wing friends who make me feel spineless for not standing up for the middleclasses whom they now call "the new poor".

It would be so much easier to live in a place where the deprivation is tucked out of sight, someplace where I am not daily confronted with these pulls; to go the whole hog and live solely among my so-called peers who have cars and jobs and mortgages. Or perhaps I should obey the dictates of my conscience, give it all away and drag my boys to live like Fr McVerry with the homeless in Ballymun?

I envy those Dubliners who claim to live in a "community" and not merely in a house or a flat. Somehow, just as the word has got put among foreigners that Dublin city is pubs and the Liffey and "characters" and stout and James Joyce and U2 and Georgian buildings, it seems sometimes that everyone who actually lives in Dublin feels he or she should live in a "community" or they are missing out on some mysterious quality of life which is difficult to define but to do with solidarity, belonging, safety and cosiness. Frank McDonald and Kevin Myers, Eamonn MacThomais and David Norris and Maeve Binchy – now they're the lucky ones. They all fit in happily into communities. At least so it seems to me when I hear them talk and see them write.

In Claremont, as well as the Residents' Association, we have Neighbourhood Watch, Foroige, a Ladies' Club, an Annual Festival, a Christmas Party, a newsletter, frequent Clean-Ups. All there for the joining. But I am not a joiner. If Maeve and David and Kevin and Eamonn and Frank lived here, would they join? Is this what makes a community? Or is it people who have a lot in common? People like me, who question everything yet feel uncomfortable with every answer, don't live in a "community", if we ever did. Perhaps our parents did, our children may in the future, but somehow, we missed out.

The problem is not Claremont, it is me. On the other hand,

I suspect that there are a great number of my generation who feel the way I do, jumped a few rungs up the ladder, but feeling they don't quite belong in many other Claremont Courts throughout the city. I suppose it's sad.

GLASNEVIN CEMETERY
Michael O'Loughlin

I began commuting from Finglas into the city when I was four years old. There were no schools available in Finglas at that time, so my mother used to bring me to the bus stop and deliver me into the care of a friendly bus conductor. He kept an eye on me, and made sure that I got off at the right stop for Strand Street School. I saw nothing strange in this arrangement; I didn't regard the bus conductor as a stranger. One aspect of growing up in a working-class suburb is that you assume every man is like your father, every woman your mother. It is more than a question of neighbourliness or community, you see the world as your family. Then you grow older and discover that in the more advanced societies this is not the case. This is a heart-breaking discovery from which you will probably never recover.

Travelling from Finglas into the city, the bus has to travel along the high stone walls enclosing Glasnevin Cemetery. This was where the dead lived, a quiet suburb straggling down the hill to the Tolka river. It was a suburb of the dead among the suburbs of the living, characterised by its trees and grass, its rustic vistas, in the midst of the grey concrete streets. Over the years, I became familiar with the cemetery. My grandfather died and was buried there, and distant relatives of whom I have no living image. We visited their graves on quiet Sunday afternoons. One of our neighbours on the street was a grave-digger, who worked there. Every day he would come home, wearing a clay-coloured suit, and boots caked with grave-earth, and a broad-rimmed brown felt hat. With his squat round form and smiling red face between his hat and jacket, he reminded me of a healthy earthworm.

I came into closer proximity with the cemetery when I was

twelve years old, and started attending a school in Glasnevin. For the next five years, I traced its edge four times a day. From the upstairs window of the bus you could look down into the cemetery, at the rows of headstones stretching into the distance. A friend once told me that, as the bus sped from Finglas into town, he looked down and glimpsed his own name, which was a very uncommon one, written on a stone. Perhaps unwisely, he returned to look for it one day, unsuccessfully. For me, going to school in Glasnevin was not just a literal displacement, but one in time and culture. It was an exile, a five year sentence to a gulag archipelago of the spirit. In one sense, Finglas could be defined in terms of absences, but it was also full of life and possibilities, the thousands of children on its streets were emblems and bearers of a kind of hope. The schools were crowded and noisy, but they were guided by a talented generation of progressive-minded teachers. I left this raw, invigorating air to be delivered into the hands of a nineteenth-century establishment, a slaughterhouse of the sensibilities, a wilderness of discipline and religion. Its aims were clear: to produce a class of Catholic civil servants, teachers, doctors. It was about power. It was also a linguistic displacement. Although they had all been born in the surrounding suburbs, they sometimes spoke with country accents, and sometimes in Irish, a badge of caste, a denial of the city I came from. Architecture, wrote Nietzsche, is the rhetoric of power, and I could hear what Glasnevin was saying to me, with its solid red-brick houses tightly grouped around defiantly ugly churches. These were the people who had triumphed, who had added the halfpence to the pence and prayer to shivering prayer till they had built a country in their own image. I never entered their houses without sensing something rotting and damp, every house seemed to contain something which had died a long time ago, and never been taken out. Years later, I came to live in one of these houses. One night we found a strange parcel hidden behind one of the shutters, probably left there by the Catholic spinster who had died shortly before we came to occupy the house. It was wrapped in a pair of old nylons, stained with something which could have been blood. When we opened it, gingerly, we found a few hundred old and disintegrating pound notes, mixed with holy pictures and relics. It was almost too apt, a metaphor made flesh.

Just across from the school was the main entrance to the cemetery, and a large grey wall equipped with watchtowers to guard against the body snatchers who once haunted it. Every day, I saw the hearses drive through the gates. The big clock above the gates ticked out the minutes of my life as I came and went from Finglas. Someone, perhaps in 1966, had painted in big white letters on the wall: *EIREÓIMÍD ARÍS*. It became something of a catchphrase in the school, but the joke was not immediately obvious to us. We sat in class and analyzed "The Windhover", but no one saw fit to tell us that its author lay in the earth a few hundred yards away, an outlandish stress in the long lines of the dead.

I left school and left Finglas, and my early commutings became a rehearsal for future displacements. But I was surprised to find that Glasnevin cemetery which had always been such an oblique, if huge, presence in my mind, had somehow become central to my thoughts. I had become a haunter of cemeteries, scrutiniser of stones, a connoisseur of their poetry. I went back to look at Glasnevin Cemetery, but it was as if I had never seen it before. It lay spread out before me like a printed text, which I had learned to read, all my life I had been carrying this book, whose contents I somehow knew. Now my eyes could pick out the pathetic pomp of the bishops' tombs, my ears were attuned to the ironies of the Republican Plot. Here was the official story of Ireland, laid out in sentences and paragraphs of stone, from the phallic pun of O'Connell's monument and the surrounding crypts, each figure carefully selected and placed in his niche, the *mot juste*, to celtic crosses commemorating some obscure writer of patriotic ballads.

But beyond this, around this, another story begins. This one is silent. Tens of thousands of graves, some almost vanished without trace, some whose names you can just decipher, with their dates. Here and there you can find a simple cross of wood without a name, or a wordless stone, with perhaps in front of it, a dusty plastic flower in an old milk bottle. There are patches of bare earth covered with fine, hair-like grass, where graves used to be, now vanished, silent forever. Here are buried the people who built the city, who worked in it and died, and were wiped out of history, leaving nothing behind but their children, perhaps, or an intonation, a verse in an anonymous song. I thought of how they must have laboured and suffered, and what the hopes were which kept them alive, and if they had been justified. I compared their silence to the rhetorical stones I had just seen. I stood there, my thoughts mired in bitterness and frustration, when an image came into my mind, one I recognised but had almost forgotten.

Somebody had once shown me a book he was translating from the Serbo-Croat, about a group of people called the Bogomils. Originally, the Bogomils were a sect which was widespread throughout the Balkans from the tenth century onward. It was a neo-Manichean heresy which spread like wildfire among the peasants and ruling class alike. Eventually, it was stamped out, as an international movement, but survived among the peasants in the backwaters of what is now Yugoslavia, until at the end of the fourteenth century, when it was absorbed into Islam. What is known about this obscure sect is that it mingled Manichean ideas with a radical social approach. They avoided all outward show, had no priests, no churches, no books, no painters. They would have vanished from history if it weren't for one thing. Scattered across the plains of Bosnia and Herzegovina, they left enormous, mysterious necropoli, suburbs of the dead. The significance of these is not clear to commentators. They consist mainly of simple blocks of stone, arranged randomly on the earth, some of which carry unsophisticated but enigmatic carvings. They often show groups of people doing ordinary things, such as dancing, or hunting. Looking at photographs of these stones, I felt a strong sense that they were telling me something about myself which I couldn't quite grasp. But the images became embedded in my memory, waiting for the right moment to reveal their significance. Standing in Glasnevin Cemetery, an image came back to me from the Bogomil tombs. It was a crude carving of a man facing the viewer, with an enormously enlarged hand raised up, palm outward. Some commentators have traced this gesture back to ancient Persian religions. But now it seemed to me to be exactly what it seemed: a hand raised in greeting and benediction, hail and farewell, a message of peace from the dead to the living. I realised that you can deprive people of everything, their rights, their hopes, their selves, but you cannot deprive them of their death, which is theirs inalienably. Standing among the Bogomil graves of Glasnevin, I felt that their silence was a message more benevolent, more hopeful, than any rhetoric. For me, Glasnevin Cemetery will always be the green, secret heart of Dublin.

MOUNTJOY SQUARE, 1974
Sebastian Barry

One evening I took a stroll through the old house in Mountjoy Square where I was living in a flat, poking into dead rooms, toeing odds and ends of boxes and drawers. You could walk a big dog through a place like that and count it exercised. No one else was in; or maybe the scholar who lived upstairs was picking over some page of Joyce above, silent and mesmerized. And I felt that sense of other lives, I saw clearly, separately, the old browness of the paint that was no longer paint in the halls, but a ghost, a coffin-coloured remnant of true paint. I heard the steps, the countless steps, the privacy of those roomkeepers going out for whatever private purchases into the greater city.

Dark winter as always, the late day full of gloom outside the windows, every object I saw beginning to speak its story, to clamour to be heard, to explain, to detail disaster and the victory of sudden joys. Each old table had been picked and purchased new once, pennies pinched to have it, each door had been opened and shut a million times, by twenty generations in as many ragged fashions. Now no one was there to disturb the hinges and they creaked with that complaint.

The lower landing was readying up for revelation, for a tiny information to me, a preparation, a hint at the very stuff of life and the use of a life. I wandered into the most battered room of the house where there wasn't even a frame in the window, only a jagged sheet of thick plastic over the hole, and the night wind icing in, and the streetlamps forward and blunt in the debris.

Here was a little tin box. I prised it open with a nail and took out a piece of old blue writing paper, the sort I used to write to my father on when he was away in London, old blue paper folded a few times into a small irregular shape. It had the dirt outside of something often handled but less often unfolded, as if it had been taken from spot to spot, extracted from book to niche to tin, over the span of a life. So settled in its folds it was almost difficult to open it.

The surface inside looked quite crisp and new, as if it had just been written on, and the writing was in a fresh pencil. The paper spoke, you could hear its voice, in the list of names and the few bleak sentences:

In this room on the night of January the 2nd the coldest night of the year we went to bed all hale, and awoke to find three of our number dead,

Jamie (Brown) aged 7 Mary and Christie Finlay, 3 months, 11 years from a suffocation. And the rest not much better

Under this, there was an entry in a different hand, or the same hand at a different time, a tireder hand perhaps, listing two others, two of the old ones, who had died

we suppose from the late effects of the same cause.

I, Jane Finlay, mother, write this down, the names of our loved ones. We must never forget this.

What was to be done with such a discovery? What did it mean? When I was long gone out of that house I used to think of that room, think of that family sleeping there in the great privacy, the secrecy of poverty, and that coldest night of the year, and that woman of the elegant words writing down the record of the event. This was her Book of Kells, her illuminated text. Still sticking to it in that dreadful room were the ribbons of their lives, the faintest sounds spiralled around the note, vague faces appeared under the force of such a signal, the small corpses of her children, the big corpses of her elders. One morning in winter — and when was this, the twenties, the thirties, the sixties? — she had awoken to find half her family suffocated, all the air in the stifled room used up. The cold absences of that day! Even now seventeen years later that note, a few words in pencil, affect me more than many a fine book has, many an excellent and resplendent play.

I suppose I was the first person to read that piece of notepaper since the last hand belonging to it had passed away from the world so thoroughly that even it, a precious document, an heirloom, a history, had not been safekept. It had lain in its tin box for decades in a room of rubble — the scholar above poring over his Joyce — its tiny message silent, waiting for a foolish student to wander about the deserted house.

I'm sure I took it with me, stuffed it in my jacket. I'm sure I took it with me out of that room and I'm equally sure I lost it. Not in safe hands! Or at best it sits among old papers of mine in some old box in my mother's house, waiting for a fresh reader, a second hearer, a better seer. I hope Jane Finlay died a nicer death than her people did that night, when it got so cold, and they stopped up the window with rags, that fine old Georgian window, and minute by minute their lungs used up the precious air, and warm enough they died, and cold she awoke, to rise, and shake her dead, and write her note.

CHILDHOOD IN ABERCORN ROAD AND SEVILLE PLACE
Peter Sheridan

The abiding memory is water. The river where men worked and the sweat that removed dependence on charity and the pawnshop. Great mountains of timber that provided a million hiding places and as many splinters, and on good days ankle deep in corn that you could crack with teeth if they were strong enough, or just suck till the heart trickled like sherbet and hit the back of the throat. And cranes, always, and swinging barges, and winch men, and occasionally, though not often enough for blood loving jacks, the rat catcher and his brew of the boiled female, the hot blood causing the primeval scream and scurry of "millions" to the menstrual bait and a watery grave in cages specially built.

In the evening the cattle boat opened its hatches. When the live animals had been shunted to their abode in the lower reaches (how they survived the flailing blows from a thousand "cattlers" or would be "cattle men" was God's design), then the human cargo poured from the pubs along the "wall", Byrne's, Campion's, The Liverpool, and clutching their faded brown cases held together with twine and their second or third class singles to Manchester, Birmingham or London, they waved to crying wives and bewildered children promising a speedy return.

The boarding of ships was forbidden in Sheridan family law — malevolent sailors, drunken captains and secret caverns leading to instant death were just some of the prohibition warnings. Younger brother John's exploit in having the cattle boat redocked (due to his unwanted presence on board) led to the unshakable family lore that his arse to this day still sports the marks of the blackthorn stick that beat his journey from the gang plank home to number 12.

When we crossed the bridge to Seville Place, an expanding family making the move from the 3 roomed Abercorn Road imperative, another waterway came to dominate - the "naller" (Royal Canal). Frozen in winter and a public baths in Summer is how it is etched in my memory. I can still see James Mulally disappearing beneath the ice and our impotence as we ran back and forth trying to break the grey ice cover with our fists to find him. Later on it claimed two members of another family, the Kavanaghs from St Brigid's Gardens. They lost another child beneath a lorry in Sheriff Street. Their particular streak of blond hair I have never seen since, nor will I again, anywhere.

In summer all thought of death was buried as we raced from the North Wall side in a great splash to the broken ship on the far East Wall bank. We travelled many times around the world in that ribbed shell.

When the swimming became proficient and the broken ship became nothing but a broken ship again, we left the little kids to paddle in the Canal while we took on the heady current of mother Liffey. Those first tentative sorties from the bottom steps soon gave way to dives, flips, and back somersaults from the bank opposite the cobble stones and horse trough of Guild Street. And if the "captain" was in good form, and you possessed sufficient bravery, a dive from the Corpo ferry meant instant exaltation to a special league of heroes. But the ultimate test was the jump from Butt Bridge to the shadows of the Loopline Bridge and the long swim to the steps at the Custom House. Many times I saw that cause cars to make involuntary stops and men and women to clap, though there was no audience to hear. To this day I regret that I never made the jump. Oh, the unfulfilled exploits of youth.

And if water dominated play, then blood replaced it at school. Blood, as in definition of manhood, jackeen, Irishman, Christian. In its ideal state that blood should produce a Gaelic speaking and Gaelic loving youth; one who enjoyed to excess the exploits of our native games, by definition loathed all foreign ones (they had a ban just in case the blood was contaminated), a man who would see the reunification of his

80

country while living and working in England (you couldn't pay for a flight to America with blood in those days) and who would shun pagans as they lay in bed on Sunday Mornings and get up to go to mass.

My blood was severely diluted. I captained Sheriff Utd F.C. from under 11 and took my responsibilities seriously. That meant not turning out for the school gaelic team. The tension of the situation became so bad that I confronted the CB concerned. I asked him what he had against soccer? He paled. He asked me did my father know I was such an insolent brat? I persisted, what was wrong with soccer, a game like any other? I was told I would have to take my bag and baggage and go elsewhere. I played my final ace. The man Gal, who runs our team was studying to be a priest, so what could be wrong with playing for the team. The CB stared me straight in the face and said, "Judas was an apostle".

Every play I've written has been an attempt to emulate that riposte.

GIMME SHELTER
Flatland
Aidan Murphy

Karl Marx once wrote that the three basic prerequisites of civilised living are food, shelter and love. The hunger and search for both food and love can have its sticky, and often painful moments, but, since I first left home in 1971, the problem of shelter has been particularly thorny - a helter-skelter of highs and lows ranging from English country mansions (with high tea at the vicarage of course) to derelict chippers not miles away from the sacrosanct White Cliffs of Dover.

I came to Dublin for the first time in 1987 on a one-way ticket and a hundred punts, and for the first two weeks crashed with friends, first in Templeogue, a bland place with about as much character as Roger Moore, and later in Phibsboro, which was brash and lively and much more to my taste.

Then, through the grapevine, I heard of a possible room in a house in the North Circular Road, and one wet evening in January I caught a 10 bus to the Phoenix Park terminus. At this stage I was fairly desperate for a room of my own - even the kindness of strangers and friends falls short of the desire for privacy and space, and a curious mixture of embarrassment and powerlessness soon sets in when one is temporarily landed in another's household.

Immediately I saw the house I had a good gut-feeling, an old redbrick three-storey, furtive behind its hedge and garden, a vision of heaven to someone with nowhere to go. I introduced myself to the first-floor tenant and waited with him in his room for my appointment with the landlord whom I had telephoned earlier. Everything in his high-ceilinged draughty room was somewhat shabby and lopsided, carvings and

83

furnishings from another century, heavy dustladen drapes, but on that January night it seemed womblike and comfortable. It was my first hint of the sensation of living underground that would return again and again over the following years. The honeycomb structure of flatland.

The landlord arrived with a clanking of keys (now a familiar sound seldom welcomed with glee) and we met. He was a garrulous man and friendly enough, but beneath the exterior I sensed a shrewd no-nonsense efficiency – the badge of the man of property. (He owns three houses in the area. I remember one dismal night in March when rent-money was scarce and the larder as good as bare he showed me a catalogue for The Boat Show. The poor man was in a quandry over what type and size of boat to purchase for the family). That first night though he showed me a room on the lower landing. Bela Lugosi would have adored it! It was a kingsize coffin with a window that was painted shut forever. "And here you have your breakfast grill", he announced, pointing into the right-hand corner at a misshapen monstrosity coiled in wires that looked about as safe as Mount Etna in a heatwave. "How much is it?" I asked, knowing how little cash I had left. "Fifteen pounds a week," he said. What could I do? I was up against a dark night and an apologetic trip back to some friend's house or I could accept this large box, for a week or two anyway until I found something better. I was on the verge of agreeing to the travesty when he said, "I can show you another room if you like." And like a potential vampire rescued in the nick of time I lapped at his heels up to the first floor.

It was perfect. At least ten or twelve times the dimension of the other, with a decent-size (and working) window and a very attractive open fireplace. I plunged into the question of rent. "This is more expensive of course," he said, (my heart sank), "this would be sixteen pounds a week." I could hardly believe it – a measly extra quid for the difference between sheer hell and tolerable limbo.

That was my first delightful introduction to the quirky

politics of rent, and the comically absurd vagaries of flat life. In this world, for instance, The Plumber is The Carpenter. He's also The Electrician and The Decorator depending on what repairs need doing. If the faucets are leaking he's The Carpenter. If the wiring is dodgy he's only The Decorator. And so on to an infinity of inaction.

During my first week living here I woke up one morning to a strange cacophany. Where the hell am I, thought, and what's going on. The morning was full of the cries of wild animals, what sounded like monkeys chattering, hippos yawning, and flocks of tropical birds screeching and yammering. The experience was a bit freaky until I discovered that I had Dublin Zoo practically in the back garden. It's nice to wake up in the tropics on a gloomy Dublin day. At night I have a light-show on my walls from the red and blue security lights of the Garda HQ. And something else...The restful sound of passing trains. The sound puzzled me when I first heard it, I presumed it was made by police helicopters. But no. I bought a map of the city and studied it carefully and found the answer. A railway line running through the park, under the People's Garden, under the Wellington Monument, to Clancy Barracks. Mysterious freight indeed for the imagination!

In this murky world of rented rooms nothing must be touched or altered. The wallpaper must peel from the walls. The dampness must spread, and the general condition of the house must deteriorate. You are aware of your impermanence. You are a transient like so many others up and down the street, and you can hear through the walls the endless buzzing of the hive, their music, their lovemaking, their quarrels, their isolation. I like it. Fourteen years in the city of London hardens the arteries to the anonymity of life, and if it is present here where I am now it is to a lesser degree. People may still be living lives of quiet desperation, with nothing much to call their own, but the mood of the community is cool and friendly. Struggle imparts its own wisdom.

So don't speak to me yet of mortgages and homeowning. The future may be open but I've always been a day-to-day man and this shelter suits me fine. I have my books, my music, my work and my privacy. I also have cupboards over my sink that would collapse under the weight of a bag of sugar. And a makeshift set of drawers that will not open more than two inches as the entire thing seems to be nailed up from the inside. It is the classical surreal object, without function or explanation. Sometimes I invite people in to view it.

FATIMA MANSIONS
Francis Stuart.

Thresholds! When we meet one we must cross it, not just the poet or the explorer, but many more "settled" and otherwise complacent people. Whether exterior or inward, we both long for and dread new adventures and experiences. A large proportion of holiday-makers are impelled by such an urge. Wandering through foreign cities we are conscious of missing thresholds that could lead to outlandish places and doings beyond the defined limits of tourism.

Such a visitor to Dublin will probably miss all of these. But so may we, so journey out along the too-familiar South Circular Road towards Dolphin's Barn - evocative name! - and turn right at St. Anthony's Road. If this thoroughfare, hardly the correct description, leads anywhere, and most locals will tell you that it does not, it more or less peters out at the westerly blocks of a Corporation complex called Fatima Mansions, not so long ago notorious as a hotbed of drug-pushers.

The drug dealers are gone I believe, pushed out by the more resolute of the residents, supported, it is said, by an illegal organisation, and Fatima has evolved, not quite out of a ghetto, though it is not, never was, that in the accepted racial or sectarian sense. Almost all the members of the community, if it is not premature to call it that, are Irish and Catholic born. What they share though, and are most aware of as a bond and a burden, is their poverty.

This hardly distinguishes them from other sections of Dublin's population, but having crossed this invisible threshold, climbed a flight or two of forbidding stone stairs and, accompanied by an informed resident, entered one of the flats, we could come to the heart of the matter. For here is the vulnerable and semi-secret growth of a new, and in the world at large, unheard of spirit, one that believes that it is possible to be poor and at the same time lead a life not deprived of fulfilment and even excitment.

Groups and committees have been formed and the more usual improvements, parks, playgrounds, re-sewageing, are being planned and even got going, founded by grants from the Gulbenkian Foundation and, I think, the EEC.

These works and projects naturally meet with little or no opposition. But when it comes to raising the level of the inner or psychological level of the communal life style there are factions and frictions. Opposition, bewilderment or indifference comes from a proportion of those who see themselves as transients, passing through on their way to better things.

There are experts brought in from outside because there is probably nobody within the community with, say, a background knowledge of trends in architectural design. While this is necessary, there is a danger that an outside authority will be listened to with greater respect than an unpaid resident whose ideas are dismissed by the pragmatists and conservatives as utopian and possibly subversive (of what?). When it comes to suggestions of painting each step in the black stairwell a different colour in series of twelve to extend the games the children already play there or put frescos on the drab walls there is less response. If the word "graffiti" is used to suggest slogans, possibly those beloved of Che Guevara long ago in newly liberated Cuba, there are protests.

At one end, or rather one of the other ends, for it is a skein rather than a spectrum, are the parents of those who go in for mindless vandalism. Mindless, because it is cannabilistic and against members of the community, in particular the more vulnerable and "unrepresentative". Some of these have had their flats broken into and ransacked several times within a year. While I'm not advocating such raids on other more prosperous neighbourhoods, they would be less malicious and presumably a better outlet for frustration. And the fact that residents who own cars, no matter how old or rusted, nor visitors, dare park them in the courtyards or vicinity (I had the windows of my ancient Fiat smashed) indicates the petty terrorism that, added to the indifference, the common aspiration has to contend with.

But, as I started by imagining, sit on a winter evening in a flat of one of the undeterred "advisors", before the open fire that all "draw" so well, and in here take the place of the TV boxes of some suburban dwellings. The front door gives directly onto the brightly-lit pedestrian "street", that is the balcony where the passers-by are neighbours who never peer through windows, for here privacy is instinctively respected, even to the point of non-interference in vandalism or serious family violence.

Listen to the discussion, tentative and mixed with a depreciating humour, about how poverty need not preclude learning to draw and paint, or playing the violin, having fun (the best of which is still free), or loving and being loved.

Thus the brilliantly lit complex of Fatima Mansions towers, though mostly not above three storeys, like a beseiged fortress or the outpost of a new and age-old aspiration and hope, above Rialto.

HOME
Noel Farlane

The best cognition, the most fruitful withdrawls from reality in the cause of reflection, occur on the upper deck of a bus.

I was indulging in a most pleasant trundle down the Conyngham Road of a Saturday night recently, the trundle made the pleasanter by the investment of an hour or two in a good pub with a good pal. I looked keenly beyond the Liffey lapping and sparkling and flashing darkly, to the dim orange glow cocooning a place that appeared almost, to be on a hill.

There were summery feelings; familial warmth and acceptance, the unembarrassed solicitude of friendship, class rapport, the enjoyable collusion of comradeship, the confidence that having a base instills, because across was Ballyfermot and Ballyfermot, though physically home no longer, is the home the heart knows.

Those interminable furrows of concrete and tar so tightly planted with the squat houses were ploughed for one reason - to assemble in one place one class of people to create wealth for another class of people. The system forges the community, the community forges the family, the family forges the child and childhood sketches the borders of what we will be in our lives.

The misunderstandings, mishearings and ignorance about the *flexibility* of the meanings of words when thrown around by adults can be a puzzle for a child, and hell for a three-and-a-half foot literalist. My standard-issue Ringsend grandmother (black-shawled, small fisherman's cottage, massive ponderous clock whose tick was as loud as its chimes were doleful, abiding terror of electricity, one ulcerated leg, one tooth, two fiery eyes, three outings a year and four really good stories) kept me awake and worried at night, sardined by my two snoring brothers, by her extraordinary behaviour on Tuesday nights. She would look at the clock, recoil, snatch up the more ostentatious of the ornaments from the venerable but shining furniture and lock them in a bedroom. The radio was secreted in the outside lav. The expulsion of all visitors would be summary and ruthless.

"Hurry up in the name of Jesus, the vengeance is coming!"

I peered through the window, watched her snap off the light (never approached without blessing herself), perch herself uncomfortably on her chair's edge, clutching her flag of widowhood tightly around her (her shawl) and amend her features into an ensemble of loneliness, abandonment, alienation. She was, I felt, assuming the position, so to speak.

The Vengeance! The "New" Webster Dictionary of the English Language (International Edition) was most explicit, but what had she done? You couldn't very well ask and I didn't; I agonised and forgot, until many years later, when she was fading and ailing in her bed, I opened her door one Tuesday night to a brace of dapper gentlemen, politely fingering the rims of their pork-pie hats.

"Hello", one said."Is herself in? We're the Vincents."

"The what?"

"The Vincent de Paul. We come every Tuesday..."

Ah! The Vengeance! Embodied at last before me. The productions of solitude and poverty she had crafted weekly for the odd few bob, the bags of coal at Christmas but most of all, I surmise, the sympathy, in her guttering days, of semi-strangers.

There was another communications snare, even though I was growing wise in the ways of adults (they were all right, but needed close watching) when my mother, in the early sixties, began to motion up Ballyfermot Road and allude to "The Scheme", "the men working on The Scheme", and when the weather was foul "the poor men working on The Scheme". But this puzzler had to take its place in the queue - I was then still recoiling from a startling passage encountered in a Victorian potboiler, in which the demure heroine, adorning something called a drawing room in somewhere called Paris, while being implored by the earnest hero to flee the cruel guillotine, suddenly produces a "jewelled hand mirror" and begins to "make her toilet"! which she "completed" after a lengthy discourse, with "a sweep of her scented puff"!

I learned what The Scheme was while being dragged (dragged sweetly, but dragged) for a second visit to the health centre "dentist". I gave the clattering, bustling construction site only an absent once-over. ("There'll be shops and all sorts of things there, won't that be great?" my mother said with grim cheer) because I was feeling the need to use the drawing-room, recalling the foot-tapping queue of children with pinched faces, straining their hearing for a scream from within; recalling the chair, big, black and shiny like a hearse, being called Neil by the old man with hard translucent fingers, the gas, unconsciousness and waking to bloody pain and the rocking-horse of nausea.

I watched The Scheme grow flesh on the skeleton of its scaffolding week by week on visits to Mass in the Church of Our Lady of the Assumption, whose bare-blocked hangar coldness was eased only by the strange, solemn, sonorous tongue people switched to when they went there.

This awesome entity in the community was the lair of the funereal and fearsome Canon Daly, a bluff beefy man obsessed with his intense campaign to strangle at birth the furtive playing of foreign games on his territory. Employing the first principle of guerilla attack, surprise, he would materialise blackly from among the boles of trees near playing fields or from the cover of parked cars in cul-de-sacs to ensure that the national mettle was not being softened through perfidious indulgence in soccer. Exchanges in his confessional, it was said after the furtive business was transacted dwelled more on the fate of Kerry Seniors than the faith of Ballyfermot's minors.

In the middle and late Sixties, already debilitated by an ulcer of poverty at its core and punished by a dearth of facilities, the media branded Ballyfermot violent. Deprivation always finds violence as the accessible expressive art and as well as the usual

93

number of weekend artists, there was an established elite of very dedicated fulltime artists, ruthless in the pursuit of carving a niche, and anyone they considered to be in the way, which would make them supreme in their calling.

Theirs was seldom the violence that broke like a wave from the front door of a pub, the crowd ducking and writhing like the body of a single animal. Trapped in their image, they "called" each other like gunfighters and met, with their hangers-on, and occasionally more than once, at predetermined rendezvous.

As well as feeding their strange addiction to the fear that they instilled the smell of ready violence which they carried also had its financial advantages - they were prized bouncers locally, willing to go where no (off duty) policeman had gone before. Their breed is fading now. This is not because peace has erupted, or that economic oppression has ceased to fuel crime or the release sought through physical force, but because there's too many people with access to guns for even the hardest of hard men to continue to indulge themselves. And even the most gratuitous bully is now aware, for those small of stature who are members of the tiny but growing community of the preying violent, for the man who has everything but the height and the weight the gun is now de rigurrier.

And there was the other kind of fight which could almost not be matched for the coldness of primal passion, when the confusion of polar emotions burst into white-hot flame - when bloody father and bloody son spilled out of an overcrowded house on to a deprived street propelled by frustration and want, having at each other with the silent intentness of assassins.

The police at that time felt quite unemcumbered when dealing with Ballyfermot people. I nursed a childhood recollection of standing outside the famous Gala Cinema (then the only recreational facility and not a bad place if you didn't mind the occasional sudden rat in the aisle) one smoky dusk as six suspects were being marched to a paddywagon after a fight inside which even the still celebrated, much-loved much stabbed "Commissionaire", Harry the Hippo, couldn't put down.

While it was horrifying to watch the casual boredom with which the cop standing at the back of the wagon batoned each in turn before projecting them inside, more horrifying was the meekness with which they accepted it.

The first feelings of deep insult at the wasting pestilence of very severe poverty were experienced in the Model School, Inchicore, a 19th-century edifice clad in grey stone, with the squat solidity of a fortress but a not unhappy, businesslike place (if you didn't mind the occasional sudden rat under the cupboard where the stick was kept). The majority of the kids scuttled down from Ballyfermot; no-one could accuse them of being privileged but neither were they destitute - they were coping working-class kids with their arses sometimes out of their hand-me-downs, busted shoes, who wouldn't use handkerchiefs when God had provided them with a good right forearm and who violently denied that their mothers gave them margarine. Such things do not scar when they are more or less the norm.

But there was an isolated minority, a self-contained tribe almost, a slightly raved coterie of kids who staggered out into the world from the most pitiless slum in the country, Keogh Barracks in Inchicore. This glowering, rat-eaten hulk was a former British Army billet, long since demolished, or maybe it just collapsed of its own evil. They gave their addresses as "Married Quarters" or "Single Quarters". It marked them. They were uniformly small and thin, many were cross-eyed and all frenetic. They shivered in the frost-covered schoolyard (when they showed) and at all times looked at food with a sexual intensity. They were skilled exponents of the fearless, stagger inducing head-butt.

When they were on the run from police, parents or territorial rivals, they hid in the hollow of a swamp not far from the school, where I went to split my school lunch with them ("Fuck that, banana sambos again."). One, who may be called Larry, I got on well with. Even then, he carried himself with the hunched, stooped attitude of the hunted. The next time I saw that unmistakeable squint unchanged by adulthood, it was fixed on me from the slits of a jauntily-coloured balaclava. His legman was getting most demonstrative with a lumphammer while cleaning out the till of the packed Sunday night public house. The drinkers had collapsed into rigidity and silence; the only movement among them was a terrified slow-motion blinking and ascending cigarette smoke. Larry's turned eye graced me with an almost imperceptible wink and, in deference to old favours, he pointed his freshly-oiled webley (I could smell it) elsewhere.

He was arrested some months later in relation to more grave matters, after, I was informed, Ballyfermot's "best shaggin car chase ever." (The informant might have added potentially murderous). "He was going around and around The Scheme with three carloads of them after him and everyone standing outside the pubs with their gargle in their hands watching the show. He turned over outside the church there. They really laid into him when they collared him, but sure he was asking for it."

Some of the victims of Keogh Barracks came to live in Ballyfermot after their hell was razed. I happened on Larry's little brother in the seventies in our recently won community centre there (in some ways it had displaced that awesome hangar down the road, that former lair of Canon Daly, as the core of the community). There had been a surge of awareness, activity, pride and organisation, but it was political only in the very broadest sense. A group had engaged itself in questioning the punishing illiteracy rates among the area's children and their skepticism towards reading and books. The riotously irrelevant content of the books disseminated to young children to nurture in them a desire to read was powerfully obvious (the flower-gardened cottage fronted by the pristine car; mummy in frilled apron, mouth forever frozen in a rictus of love and domestic satisfaction and appearing to be in the saddest stages of anorexia; besuited Father with implanted pipe, wielding a briefcase; floral little Jane surgically attached to an

96

apple-cheeked doll and enthusiastic Dick, constantly outshone, alas, by the dullest of dogs called Spot.)

A lot of working-class children and others, I'm sure, were being Mummyed, Fathered, Dicked, Janed and Spotted into a particular attitude. There was also the matter of the rebellion against the act of imagining (if your world is a tough world, you have to keep attuned relentlessly or something's going to hammer you.) It was decided to produce an appropriate book for the children. This was achieved, and to my great personal contentment, became very widely robbed.

It was in the course of soundings among the children that I met Larry's little brother (introductions unnecessary for my part, he was Larry's clone, right down to the turned eye.) He did me a considerable and self-taxing favour by flicking through a typical Dick and Jane confection, anxiously tapping a plastic-sandalled foot. Well, what did he think of it? He gave it all he had, his full 12-second attention span.

"Imagine having a dyin-lookin fuck like that for a da?"

He exploded from the door, all interest lost shouting for his mates. Message received.

As the system forges the community, so it can butcher it. It would be facile to term Ballyfermot in these times as a community under assault, economically and as a propaganda target (this enfilade of propaganda succeeds when the unemployed man vegetating on a street corner rounds on un-married mothers) because it is not under attack as a communi-ty, it is under attack as a class. The importation, fully assem-bled, as it were, of the social death-machine of monetarism has turned the ulcer of want and demoralisation into a galling cancer.

Every ill and anchor that afflicts Ballyfermot springs from the current economic arrangement. The only door to hope is through rearrangement. Recovery is not on the agenda in monetarism; it is a mechanism which sharpens, realigns and then consolidates social division.

Trundling down the Conyngham Road, looking keenly at the orange glow of streetlights across the river, a certain thought kept the reflection pleasant and unbroken by undue despair – that a spirit of political resistance can find heart and head and hand and maybe enough people will combine to remark: "Imagine having a dying-looking creed like that for a system?"

KICK THE CAN
Fintan O'Toole

The thin steel cut into the ice, like a knife into a wedding cake, sending invisible furrows of white powder to each side of the skate. Billows of smoke rose towards the ceiling of the church, insense scented charcoal, as the altar boy swung the thurible. Squeals of delight echoed round the cold quarry as the children hurled themselves over the frozen surface of the bottomless pit. Murmurs of prayer ascended with the steam from their wet coats, and the priest prepared to raise his hands in benediction. There was one crack and then two screams as the children disappeared into the open mouth of the ice. Murmurs of unease rippled through the congregation as the priest was called from the altar and returned to mount the pulpit steps, his face set in plaster like a death-mask. A last glimpse of a small hand vanished, sucked into the dark, relentless water. "Go home" said the priest "and check on your children. There has been a terrible accident in the quarry pool."

These images threatened the tranquillity of the morning as we wound our way round the edge of the cycle track, a hollow in the middle of the park that had once been the quarry pool and was now officially called Eamonn Ceannt Stadium in memory of one of the leaders of the 1916 Rising. I saw it now, its grey tarmacadam sides sloping outwards like the ashen rim of an extinct volcano and remembered it as it had been a few weeks before splashed with the roaring red jerseys of the Russian cyclists, red as erupting lava, bringing that same volcano to life. I remembered the wonder of that evening, those exotic red centaurs, half-men, half-machines, making the whole cycle track spin like a whipped top as they hurtled round, suspended at impossible angles by invisible wires of centrifugal force.

And I remembered, too, going home that evening and telling my mother where I had been and she remembering the night she had been on retreat in the church and the priest announcing the terrible news about the children drowned in the quarry. I touched the wire of the fence surrounding the track and found it cold against my clammy fingers, much colder than the summer morning air.

We were going through the estate of Crumlin on our way to Terenure to find bamboos. There was something awesome about a bamboo, its feel as smooth as a bleached white bone, the incredible contrast between its innocent weightlessness in the hand and the burning sting it could deliver to the flesh, the way it could divide the very air with a singing whish. Bamboos had grace and danger and we desired them that summer with a maddening lust. Johnny Connolly, who had assumed leadership of our shifting, ill-defined gang, said that he had seen bamboos in the garden of a big house in Terenure and that morning we fell into line for the expedition.

Johnny had the authority of absence. For eight days once he had disappeared from home and school. His picture had been printed in the evening paper, along with a description of the clothes he had last been seen wearing and a request to contact the police. His absence had hung about the place like a lost dog. True, kids often disappeared, a few dying, a few emigrating, but mostly just sent to Letterfrack or Artane for mitching school or knocking off a few pence. They would vanish, the word of where they had been sent would spread, and they would return, quieter, sneakier, more vicious. But Johnny's missing days were more mysterious, redolent as they were of a thousand dark possibilities. Fantastic rumours had been traded in the park shelters: he had been ritually murdered by satanists in the Hell Fire Club, which we could see clearly in the hilly distance; he had done a bunk with the poor box out of the chapel; and there was something about girls which I had to pretend to understand. Eventually, a man in Bray recognised him and he was sent home. His refusal to say anything about what he had done and where he had gone was so absolute that by now we had given up asking. But when he suggested going to look for bamboos, there was no one, not even one as timid as me, who could resist.

I did not think it consciously as we trailed through the estate, through the winding, treeless monotonous roads flanked by rows of identical little houses in blocks of four or eight, dodging children playing Beds with shoe polish boxes for piggies, and dogs that might dart out of occluded gateways, but we were children of a new wilderness. We were city kids but our games were different from those of our parents who grew up nearer to the city centre. We could play football on the roads. We could use Alsatians to hunt rats in the dank darkness under the canal bridges. We had a game specifically invented for the narrow roads of the estate, where you threw a ball from the path on one side and scored a point if it ricocheted back into your arms off the sharp edge of the opposite path. By growing up where we did we were different from them, though we shared something of their sense of loss.

Like us that day, our parents had been explorers, though for the most part involuntary ones, cast adrift without map or compass, deprived of familiar co-ordinates, thrust, as Jim Larkin put it in 1939 "into areas to which they are not acclimatised". "They are simply dumped down there; they don't understand their surroundings. No one ever goes near them except to collect the rent". To many the very air that they breathed in Crumlin seemed literally alien and dangerous. Larkin complained that people with tuberculosis were being put into Crumlin and ran a campaign on behalf of a man who had been allocated a house in Lismore Road even though he had TB: "The atmosphere there was such that this man with TB could not stand it." To the planners, the fresh clean air of Crumlin was to be a blessing for the labouring classes after their confinement in the grimy atmosphere of the city centre, but for the poor who were planted in Crumlin the reality was different. "A lot of people" admitted Dublin Corporation's

Allocations Officer Thomas Burke in 1939 "declare that the air is so strong that the children eat them out of house and home. They cannot afford to keep the children in food. They would prefer to go back to any place out of it."

If even the air was an alien element, Crumlin had little history or legend to locate yourself by, and what it had belonged to those other than our parents' tribe, the Catholic Irish, to invaders and aliens, outlanders and outlaws. The invading Partholans settled here and buried their plague victims nearby. Oisin, not the vigorous hero of the Fianna, but the dying returned exile, shaking his head and mumbling about the changed times, had lived here, alone, afraid confused. King Billy had issued a proclamation prohibiting the use of brass money from Crumlin, an act still celebrated in the oath of the Orange Order, but celebrated only by the infidel protestant. *Holinshed's Chronicles* had described the rabble of Crumlin as a "lobbish and desperate clobberiousness". Such scraps of esoteric history, even had they known them, could not have served as fixed co-ordinates for Crumlin's new people, disparate, desperate, uprooted and ungrateful as they were.

We straggled along Sundrive Road. Here the planners who had ordained this place had performed their first act of faith, animated by a naive belief in word magic. They had taken a serpentine mud track called The Dark Lane and transformed it by the power of words into Sundrive Road, a nomenclature that summoned up the beatific bourgeois vision of happy families out for a jaunt on a sunny Sunday afternoon, a propitious place to build the houses for the first ninety families to occupy in 1935. On moving in, they found that other Victorian visions had come into play: houses specifically designed for very large families had just two small bedrooms, and yet the designers had seen fit to take up precious space with that most Victorian of bourgeois domestic ideals - a parlour. ("Somewhere" and old lady told me "to bring the insurance man for a chat when somebody died".) Nor could the planners bring themselves to see the houses as places of work: the kitchens were combined with the main living area, leaving the working women with no space of their own and large families under their feet. "Somebody told me," said Dominic Behan, who lived on Kildare Road, "that the man responsible for their design committed suicide. I'm quite sure his death, if at all, was accidental, for no man with a mind like his could ever succeed in anything so calculated as taking a life, even his own."

The Crumlin through which we made our way was an intemperate remark, not fully uttered before being deeply regretted. Conceived in panic, born of haste, and raised in rueful dismay, Crumlin was not fully built before officials and institutions were already talking of it as a mistake. Within a year of the first families moving in, the Society of Saint Vincent de Paul had issued a urgent appeal, stating that many of Crumlin's tenants had great difficulty in affording the rents, as well as additional busfares and that this had caused "serious reduction in the amount of food which could be bought". "Many families find it impossible under present conditions to live, save on a level that amounts practically to starvation." A District Justice McCarthy, sentencing young men of the area, was soon to ask "Does anything good ever come out of Crumlin?" Even the City Engineer and Town Planning Officer had jointly suggested that the policy of "providing very large areas of single-class housing" should not be repeated. "It is hardly necessary to emphasise the difficulties that have resulted from this policy which has given us large areas of one-class communities as Crumlin." Hardly had they been invented when Crumlin and its people had been virtually written off and written out.

For in spite of the cheery optimism which transformed Dark Lane into Sundrive Road, Crumlin was the product more of fear and shame than of idealism. The shame lay in the fact that Independent Ireland, having blamed British neglect for the degradation of the Dublin tenements had itself, if anything, presided over a worsening in the housing conditions of the Dublin working-class. In 1913, there were 25,822 Dublin families living in conditions unfit for human habitation, making the city the scandal of Europe. In 1938, the figure was actually higher: 28,210 families, nearly 70,000 people.

And this shame bred fear, fear of disorder, fear of breakdown, fear of chaos. In 1939, Dublin Corporation's Housing Allocations Officer reported that tension over housing allocation could lead to "riots in the city": "At first, when I took over, the city of Dublin area was in a very discontented state...Members of the Council were actually knocked down." As late as 1945, the Jesuit periodical *Studies* noted that "There is in Dublin a growing population of Christians who have not succeeded in resisting the horrible pressure of rats, filth and overcrowding and who are losing, generation by generation, their traditional standards of human decency...dressed in rags, inarticulate, dirty, and often dishonest, they drift into the street corner gangs which are the despair of social workers and the concern of the police. This class of social pariahs, existing on inadequate relief...already constitutes a social danger which might easily grow to uncontrollable dimensions."

With fear, came compulsion. Most of the people who settled in Crumlin were forced to do so. Their own slum areas, zoned for clearance, were demolished, the Corporation fulfilling its obligations by shifting the people to Crumlin. For the Corporation, houses in Crumlin cost just six hundred pounds each to build, compared to nine hundred in the city centre. (Decent houses in Crumlin would have cost more: when the Iveagh Trust built good working-class homes in Crumlin in 1925, the houses cost them nine hundred and fifty one pounds each to build.) People were forced from slum rooms at five shillings a week in the city centre to houses in Crumlin that cost between seven shillings and sixpence and ten shillings a week. In addition there was an extra half crown busfares a week for every working member of the family, all coming from an income that was generally around two pounds and ten shillings. For a very large proportion of its population, therefore, Crumlin was an immediate disaster, a calamity that

Thomas Burke of the Corporation "that if we have to clear an area, none of the families will go outside the area. There may be an odd family that will go out to Crumlin." Of those who did not want to go to Crumlin "in most of these cases we decide they have to go off to Crumlin."

The degree of compulsion is clear from the Corporation's own surveys of its tenantry. A survey in the late thirties of 20,000 families living in overcrowded accommodation in the city centre – people who were, therefore, living in desperate conditions – which offered them houses in Crumlin and Larkhill as the "only two schemes in which they would have any chance" of Corporation housing, got a total of 360 applicants for Crumlin and 200 for Larkhill. "That means" concluded Burke "that at the present moment those people in the city do not want to go to Larkhill or Crumlin at all."

And acquaintance with Crumlin did nothing to assuage the feelings of being in internal exile. In 1939, just four years after the first tenants moved in, Burke was forced to admit that 400 of the 2,000 families had actually applied to be transferred back to the city centre. "We did not grant any at all." And even this figure of 20% of the population which was prepared to move back to slum conditions was a gross underestimate. "To others who would apply we would say "it is no use in applying unless you get someone else to exchange". If we were to circularise the Crumlin tenants, and ask them how many would like to get back to the city, we would get a thousand applications. They would get the impression that they could get back, and a regular landslide would take place. For that reason, we avoid asking if they would like to get back." Burke was already despairing of the possibility of housing the working-class in Crumlin without outright compulsion. "They were asked would they go to Crumlin; they said 'Crumlin will do us all right'. Then they come back and say 'Crumlin would suit you but it does not suit me at all.' ... They feel out of their element, and the sooner they get back, they think, the better... we will eventually have to reach a point where we will have to force these people into these houses."

The Crumlin they created was, to a large extent, a city of children and consumptives. Families with tuberculosis and families with large numbers of children were given priority in the allocation of housing, so that these two types of maltreated humanity prevailed. And for the first fifteen years of the estate's life, before the virtual eradication of TB in the city, the consumptives infected the children. One doctor noted of Crumlin in 1945 that "persons suffering from active pulmonary tuberculosis" were "sprinkled at random throughout a community of babies, young children, and adolescents, when they were at their most infective stage and their unfortunate young neighbours at the most susceptible period of their lives. No tuberculosis dispensary, no hospital, not even a district nurse at first, were provided to mitigate this evil." And children died, their corpses added to the underground history that Crumlin was accumulating.

For those children who lived, a fine facility was provided for their future, a magnificent granite police barracks overlooking the estate, easily Crumlin's finest building until the permanent church was erected. "A fine police barracks" *Studies* noted wryly in 1945 "has been provided to control the unruly crowds of workless adolescents for whom there are no factories, no technical schools no secondary schools, no football grounds."

We left the estate and edged towards the lusher gardens, the more spacious and sedate houses of Terenure. We climbed walls, jumped over streamlets, crawled through thickets, Johnny taking us over some unknown terrain that skirted the back gardens of the rich. We plunged into a hollow and emerged again, then dropped over a high wall, the impact shooting a thud from my heels to my brain. This was it. We were in a loose copse of half-wild shrubs, interlaced with nettles and brambles, from which we could see, across a dipping stream and a rising bank, the whole grove of waving bamboos, their thin green plumes nodding in the breeze. We rushed through the copse, brambles tearing at our clothes, nettles injecting acid into our bare legs. We splashed through

106

the shallow muddy water and in the same movement hurled ourselves up the steep bank, where at the top a man in flannel trousers with iron grey hair stood shouting "Get to hell out of here or I'll call the police." We scattered in terror, some rolling, some jumping down the bank, and when next we recollected ourselves, we were sitting in the tall grass in the field beside the graveyard, about a mile away. We sat there shocked and disconsolate for a long time, realising as we had not done before that we might have been criminals or outlaws, that we might have gone to Letterfrack, and, worse still, that we would never have bamboos.

A few nights later, my mother had a dream. In it she saw Johnny Connolly lying in our road, his life's blood draining away, his lips mouthing the words "Help me" but no one near to save him. In the morning she told us of the dream. At lunchtime when we came home from school we heard that Johnny had died. He had broken into the dispensary the previous night and shoved handfuls of coloured pills down his throat. They found him sitting in a chair, his eyes wide open, his hand stretched out in supplication. They said it had taken him a while to die. He was the first young man in our area to die of an overdose, though some years later old women would be handing out syringes and sachets of heroin to the children at the primary school gates, and at night the pebbledashed walls of the houses were flecked by the moving shadows thrown by the torches of the vigilantes.

The afternoon at school after we heard about Johnny hung about our shoulders like an old kit bag full of troubles. The clock, its heavy case stained with the accumulated exhalations of our young years, beat out time with the threatening monotony of a Christian Brother tapping his leather in agitation upon a desk. Seven minutes past three. Ten past. Thirteen past. The teacher's voices thickened to an indistinct hum, a rumble on a faraway highway, fading into some other distance. A quarter past. I closed one eye, then opened it and closed the other, making a telegraph pole flick from one window to the next, the only moving thing on the horizon. I looked into the Jewish graveyard beside the school and the white stones stared unblinkingly back.

Below, in the schoolyard, the little kids, already free, were playing kick-the-can. You put an empty can on the ground, covered your eyes and counted while the others hid. Then, one by one, they emerged with stealth or with speed to try to kick the can. If you touched them before they could kick it over, they fell down dead and lay frozen until someone managed to kick it, and it crashed across the concrete like the last trumpet blowing. Then, like good souls on the last day, their bodies would rise again in glory. This particular guardian of the can was nimble, and already young bodies were scattered, fallen around the prize.

There was a commotion from the graveyard and its green doors swung open and a crowd first filed, and then shoved in. Old Cullen the gravedigger pressed his palms together nervously and hopped from one foot to the other as he inched backwards, afraid to turn his back on the advancing dignitaries. The crowd was pierced by the brow of a coffin as it forged through like an icebreaker, borne on the shoulders of six long, thin, dark men. And there, behind the coffin, thinner, darker, made impossibly long by the black top hat that grew out of his head like the funnel of a stately ocean liner, was Him - Dev, Eamon de Valera, the Chief, the President of the Republic. I stared in shock and disbelief and then remembered that today was indeed the burial day of Robert Briscoe, a former Lord Mayor of Dublin, an old Fianna Fail comrade-in-arms.

And as they glided silently towards the grave, I thought for some reason of the time when Brother Chalky, similarly long and just as decrepit, advancing with menace on us in the yard, had suddenly and without a sound fallen straight as a poker into an open shore, a momentary, wordless, exclamation mark. And in my daydream I saw Dev and his comrades sail majestically towards the open maw of the grave, seeing nothing in their blindness until they stumbled in and were swallowed. Down they fell, endlessly down, until the black of their clothes merged with the blackness of the earth and they were gone forever.

In the yard, a boy was gaining on the can, its guardian just behind but out of reach. I knew at that moment that he would kick it before he could be touched and that its tumultuous clatter across the concrete would awaken not just the dead of the yard, but all the dead children of Crumlin, the tubercular, the overdosed, the drowned. In the park, under the cycle track named after the hero of 1916, the ice would part again, and small hands would grasp its sides. The skaters would climb out, shake the cold drops from their backs, and go home. His foot was poised to strike and the tin can glinted in the still strong sun. "Kick the can" I shouted in my mind. "Kick the fucking can."

FRIDAY THE 13th MAY –
DOING SHARON'S DA
Gene Kerrigan

The following is a court report which first appeared in **The Sunday Tribune** *in July, 1989.*

The defendants were pleading guilty, so there was no need for a drawnout recital of evidence. The facts of the case had to be presented to the judge, Mr Justice Henry Barron, so that he had the information neccessary to decide on appropriate sentencing. Detective Sergeant Gerry O'Carroll, the garda in charge of the investigation, took the stand and told the Central Criminal Court what the case was about. Prosecuting counsel, Denis Vaughan Buckley SC, read aloud from copies of the four defendants' statements, asking D/S O'Carroll to verify that his account of the statements was accurate. There were four statements with some further elucidation of the facts by counsel and the detective and by a probation officer, on Monday last and again on Friday. From the information placed before the court the following narrative of the evidence has been constructed. All of the facts and quotations are taken from evidence and statements read out in court.

Jesse and Sharon started going together in February 1988 and about a month later, according to Jesse's statement, Sharon asked him to kill her father. Jesse O'Dwyer lived in Saul Road, Crumlin, Dublin, with his mother and brother and sister Jenny. Sharon Payne was a friend of Jenny's. She was aged 15, and she lived at 82 Rutland Grove, Crumlin, with her parents and her 13-year old brother Christopher Jr.

Jesse was born in January 1970. He lived in England and his parents were divorced when he was four, after which his mother came back to Ireland with her children. As a teenager Jesse spent some time knocking around the Birmingham area, living with relatives and in hostels, before returning to Ireland in late 1987. He had on occasion got jobs as a labourer or tyre fitter but he was mostly unemployed, with no great prospects.

In October of that year he was charged with stealing a bike. A couple of weeks later he was charged with taking a car. This was all dealt with in the Metropolitan Children's Court. A month later Jesse graduated to the District Court, charged with burglary. He got probation. It was all smalltime stuff. A couple of months later he started going with Sharon Payne.

Sharon's father, Christy Payne, aged 52, didn't like Jesse O'Dwyer and tried to end the relationship between Jesse and Sharon. One reason was that there were nights Jesse used climb up onto the roof of the kitchen extension and in through the bedroom window to be with Sharon. Mr Payne had for many years suffered severe kidney failure and was physically very weak. To stay alive he had to constantly attend Beaumont Hospital for kidney dialysis.

Jesse would later tell the police that Sharon told him that her father used beat her mother, and Sharon too. His counsel, Patrick McEntee SC, told the court on Friday that for weeks Jesse resisted Sharon's request that he kill her father.

According to McEntee, Sharon then approached a friend of his, 17-year old Stephen McKeever, with the same request. According to McKeever's statement read in court, Sharon suggested ten or twelve times over the next fortnight that her father be killed. In April 1988, Jesse and McKeever burgled the Payne house and stole a TV, two videos and a camera.

Stephen McKeever was born in January 1971, he lived in nearby Drimnagh with his parents and sister. As a juvenile he had some small scrapes with the law that cost him some fines, but he had no serious record. He too was unemployed. He was known as Stitch.

In discussing the proposed killing of Christy Payne, Stitch asked Jesse what was in it for him. Stitch's statement read to the court said that Jesse told him that Mrs Payne, Sharon's mother, said she would pay Jesse £3,000 as soon as she got the insurance from the burglary.

Early on Friday 13th May 1988 Anthony O'Neill, aged 18, from Drimnagh, dropped up to Jesse O'Dwyer's house. He was friendly with Jesse's sister Jenny. Jesse O'Dwyer and Stitch McKeever were there. "I know where there's an easy touch", Jesse said. The Payne house. If there was any hassle from old man Payne Jesse would hit him a few digs. Anthony O'Neill asked Jesse if Sharon knew about this. Jesse said yes, she wanted it done, the court was told.

It would be cool, Jesse said.

Anthony O'Neill was the youngest son of a family of five from Drimnagh. When attending CBS Crumlin he played truant and began getting into trouble. In 1982, at the age of 13, he was sent to St. Joseph's industrial school in Clonmel, after being given three years detention for larceny. He was convicted in 1985 of being a passenger in a stolen car. He was sniffing glue, smoking cannabis, drinking heavily, taking pills and cider. The stuff he was on was not physically addictive but O'Neill displayed a pattern of psychological addiction. He did a number of AnCo courses but remained unemployed.

O'Neill left Jesse's house on that Friday 13 without agreeing to become involved in a burglary of the Payne house. At about 9 o'clock that evening he met a friend, Neil Kelly, also aged 18. The pair bought four cans of Holsten Pils lager from an off-licence on Sundrive Road and went to a field off the Old County Road.

There were about ten young people drinking in the field, which is known locally as The Plots. At The Plots someone gave Kelly some tablets, roches, about eight of them. Roches are named after the drug company which manufactures them, they are usually Valium. In housing estates all over Dublin, at drinking parties such as this one, kids swallow pills of indeterminate dosage, mixed with drink (usually cheap cider) to make a powerful and immediate intoxicant. Neil Kelly swallowed the roches. He was not a regular user and he became immediately spaced out.

Neil Kelly, born in November 1969, was an apprentice fitter. He had one conviction, in November 1987, for malicious damage to a car rearview mirror. He was fined £20 and ordered to pay £5 to Vincent de Paul.

On that evening of Friday 13 May, Anthony O'Neill and Neil Kelly bought another two bottles of Holsten and then the Guards raided The Plots and they had to leg it, dropping one of the bottles of Holsten. They went back to The Plots when the coppers were gone.

At about 10.30pm Jesse O'Dwyer and Stitch McKeever arrived at the Plots. Anthony O'Neill asked Jesse, "Are you still going to do that?", referring to the proposed burglary. He was well on with drink and pills himself and it seemed to him that Jesse and Stitch were a bit spaced. He said to Jesse that he didn't think they were in a fit state.

Jesse said the burglary was on and O'Neill agreed to go along. O'Neill said they'd have to take Neil Kelly as well, as he didn't want to leave him in The Plots on his own. When Jesse asked Neil Kelly if he was on for a stroke Kelly asked him how much it was worth. A few grand, said Jesse.

They went up to Jesse's house on Saul Road. Jesse explained that all O'Neill and Kelly would have to do was watch the kids and the mother after they were tied up.

No, said Kelly, he didn't want to get involved in a tie-up job. Someone gave him a roche and he took it and he didn't protest anymore. He was given a grey track suit top to wear and red and white BMX gloves.

They made ballys – balaclavas – by cutting the arms off woolen jumpers. They cut holes in the arms to see through.

They got Jesse's brother Alan to give them a lift in his white Hiace van and at around 11pm they set out, the court was told. Near Rutland Grove Alan O'Dwyer and a friend got out and the four others – Jesse O'Dwyer, Stitch McKeever, Anthony O'Neill and Neil Kelly – continued on, Jesse driving. As far as O'Neill and Kelly were concerned they were off to do a burglary. Only Jesse and Stitch knew that there were plans for Christy Payne.

As they passed the Payne house Neil Kelly, who up to now hadn't known the target, said, "That's Sharon's gaff". "I know", said Jesse, "don't worry".

They parked the van about seven houses away from the

Payne house and the four of them got out. "Yous wait there", Jesse told O'Neill and Kelly. Jesse and Stitch went towards the Payne house. There had been a stolen car around the area and a garda squad car arrived. Spotting O'Neill and Kelly waiting where Jesse had told them to wait, the cops told them to move on. The two walked down the road to a friend's house, but she wasn't in, so they moseyed back up to the Payne house.

Jesse went around the back, Stitch knocked on the front door. The other two were standing at the side of the house. They all put on their makeshift balaclavas. Neil Kelly was having trouble pulling the jumper sleeve over his head. Across the road a neighbour was staring at this carry-on. She reached for the phone and rang the garda station on Sundrive Road.

Christopher Payne, aged 13, opened the door and Stitch, O'Neill and Kelly went in. Upstairs Sharon Payne was with her friend Jenny O'Dwyer, Jesse's sister. Mrs Philomena Payne was out, and Mr Payne was at Beaumont Hospital having his blood cleaned through dialysis.

The trio, Stitch, O'Neill and Kelly, tied up Sharon and Christopher in Sharon's bedroom at the back of the house, using telephone wire. One of the gang went to keep look-out at the front window and minutes later saw the police, who had been alerted by the anxious neighbour, arriving outside. Stitch untied young Christopher Payne and told him to go down and tell the coppers everything was alright. The gang stayed upstairs and took their masks off. If the coppers came upstairs, Stitch said in his statement read in court, Sharon would tell them everything was ok.

Just then there was a tap at the back bedroom window and Jesse climbed in, using his usual mode of entry.

Young Christopher Payne told the gardai that there was nothing wrong, but they insisted on coming in and looking around. Everything appeared ok, the gardai did not go upstairs, after a few minutes they left.

At around 11.30pm Mrs Philomena Payne arrived home. When she saw what was happening she started shouting at Sharon and she was taken upstairs to the front bedroom. "You know what we're here for", she was told. Mrs Payne said they shouldn't do it. "No", she said, according to Stitch's statement read in court, "he's dying." Jesse said he wanted a word with her.

"What's the story?", he asked. Should they do it? The court was told she replied, "Do it, but be sure you get away." According to Stitch's statement she said, "Alright, but don't hurt the children. Do it quick, I don't want him to suffer."

It was now pushing midnight and Christy Payne was due home from Beaumont Hospital. Jesse kept watch at the front window for his arrival by taxi.

It finally dawned on Neil Kelly that this was more than an ordinary burglary. What's going on? he wanted to know. Someone said to him they were going to bump off the oul fella, Christy Payne.

"Me bollocks", said Kelly. "No way".

Don't worry, he was told, it's all planned, just watch them, the ones tied up.

Kelly went into the front bedroom where Philomena Payne was tied up on the floor. She was crying. "Are you alright?" asked Kelly.

"Don't touch the kids", she said.

Kelly put a pillow under her head. She asked for another pillow and Kelly got it. He lit a cigarette for her and put it in her mouth.

Kelly went into the back bedroom, to Sharon Payne. "Forget it", he said, "we're going". Kelly's statement read in court said that Sharon said, "No, no, you've got to go ahead with it. Do it! Do it!"

Kelly left the bedroom and headed down the stairs. There was a noise at the door, a key in the lock, the door opened and Christy Payne was standing there.

It was about twenty minutes past midnight when Christy Payne arrived home from his kidney dialysis session at Beaumont Hospital. "Here he is", said Jesse O'Dwyer, watching the taxi pull up outside. Neil Kelly was coming down the stairs, Jesse and Stitch were in the hall, when Christy

Payne came into the house. As soon as he saw the balaclavas he said, "Right lads, if you leave now there'll be nothing more said". The gang could see how weak he was. Jesse kicked the front door shut and told Christy Payne to get into the living room. He had no money, Payne said, he was burgled three weeks ago and everything was cleaned out.

"We don't want your money", said Jesse, "we want your life".

They bundled Christy Payne into the living room and sat him down in an armchair. Jesse had a hammer, which had been found in the house. Stitch had found a felling axe. It had a three foot long handle and the head weighed seven pounds. All four raiders stood around the seated Christy Payne. Stitch, with the axe, was standing behind the armchair.

Christy Payne kept telling them he had no money, asking them to let him be. Jesse grabbed him and pulled him up, pushed him down again. "I heard you were a child molester", he said, "and that you shoot crossbows at kids".

Stitch McKeever, standing behind the armchair, swinging the axe with both hands, brought the blade down into Christy Payne's head, splitting his skull open. Payne slumped forward and to one side. Stitch hit him again, this time with the blunt edge of the axe. Blood flowed, the skull almost cleft in two.

"He's not dead."

Jesse swung the hammer at the side of Christy Payne's shattered head. A piece of scalp flew up and stuck to the living room curtain.

Anthony O'Neill grabbed Neil Kelly and the two ran from the house. Jesse and Stitch ran out after them. They got into the Hiace van and drove off. After "doing Sharon's da", Jesse O'Dwyer later told police, they threw away the balaclavas and the hammer and went home.

The Paynes, mother, daughter and son, made statements that night about the burglars invading the house at Rutland Grove. Next morning the police showed young Christy Payne his statement and asked him if that was the truth. He talked to them again. Within hours the four members of the gang had been arrested and were being questioned. Within minutes they broke and admitted their involvement.

Christy Payne remained in a coma for several months, severely brain damaged. When he regained some consciousness he was paralysed and was not fit to be interviewed by police. He was little more than a vegetable. In November last, six months after the attack, he died. Professor John Harbison, the state pathologist, did an autopsy. He reported that Christy Payne's kidney failure was so gross that he was not prepared to say that Payne died from the injuries inflicted on him that night in May.

Charges of attempted murder were withdrawn and Jesse and Stitch pleaded guilty to charges of grievous bodily harm. O'Neill and Kelly pleaded guilty to burglary. They were due to be sentenced on Friday by Mr Justice Henry Barron.

Each defendant was separately represented by senior counsel; Jesse by Patrick McEntee, Stitch by Paul Carney, O'Neill by Vincent Landy and Kelly by John Rogers. Detective Sergeant Gerry O'Carroll was asked by each lawyer to give an account of each defendant. O'Carroll said that, unlike Jesse O'Dwyer and Stephen McKeever, O'Neill and Kelly had not been involved in violence and had immediately shown remorse for Christy Payne. He said that O'Neill is "not a hardened criminal" and in his view could be rehabilitated.

O'Carroll said that Kelly "was very much out of his head" with a combination of drugs and drink and "really didn't know what was going on". Kelly "happened to be in the wrong place at the wrong time".

Jesse O'Dwyer, said D/S O'Carroll, was "persistently asked" by Sharon and Philomena Payne to kill Christy Payne. He was "hounded", he said. Asked if anyone else had been charged D/S O'Carroll said "Not at the moment". He said that Jesse O'Dwyer resisted the suggestion of killing for some time, that he was manipulated, that he and Stephen McKeever were played off against each other, that Jesse O'Dwyer appeared to believe things he was told about how Sharon and her mother had been the victims of brutality by Christy Payne over long periods of time.

Judge Barron adjourned the proceedings until the following Thursday and asked the state counsel, Denis Vaughan Buckley, to inquire of the Director of Public Prosecutions if there were to be any further charges in this case.

When the court resumed on the following Thursday Mr Vaughan Buckley told the judge that the DPP had now directed that two other persons be charged with grevious bodily harm and with intent to murder Christy Payne, but they had not yet been arrested.

The judge sentenced both Jesse O'Dwyer and Stephen McKeever to nine and a half years in jail. Anthony O'Neill was ordered to keep the peace for three years and to undergo drug therapy at Coolmine for at least a year. Neil Kelly received a suspended sentence of eighteen months.

MARY NORRIS
Nell McCafferty

The country was shocked in July 1987, by the death of Mary Norris and her four daughters in a fire at their home in Clondalkin. Nell McCafferty had spoken to her weeks before after another fire there. Then she met a thin, wise-cracking woman who always lived on the edge of disaster. Mary Norris lost out to fate ever earlier than her friends expected. That article first appeared in **The Irish Press**.

Four weeks before her life ended, Mary Norris told me that she would welcome death. In the month succeeding that interview, those who knew her, neighbours, welfare officers and community workers alike, sensed that another disaster was approaching. They did not anticipate death, or the deaths of her four daughters.

Now that it has happened, they acknowledge, bleakly, that the circumstances of Mary's life were such that death must have seemed a release to her. She fell all the way through the welfare net. Try though they might, and many tried to help her, no one knew how. Mary moved like quicksilver on shifting sand.

At the heart's core of this wise-cracking, resourceful, childlike, childish illiterate 29 year-old woman was loneliness. "The only good thing to come out of me disasters is that the neighbours come round. I like that. I like the company," she told me.

She was, at the time, sitting at her kitchen table, talking about yet another fire in her house. While she spoke, the women were making tea, bringing in clothes collected in the area to replace those burned, sweeping up debris, washing down the sooty walls. All the electricity in the house had been switched off as a safety precaution, save that in the kitchen which Corporation workmen left functioning. Her husband, Jamesy, was up in Finche's pub.

Mary hoped *The Irish Press* would publicise her story and help her secure a bigger, brand-new house around the corner. The damage to her livingroom did not justify such a move. A coat of paint, and fresh wallpaper, and re-wiring would have left the house as habitable as it was before, though as empty as before. The furnishings were meagre. The torn wallpaper in the bedrooms and hallway had been like that before the fire of June 10, which caused the neighbours to contact this *The Irish Press*.

Another new house, another new start, would only have provided another setting for the disasters that regularly engulfed Mary's life. House-fires had already occurred in her previous Corporation homes in Blanchardstown and Ballyfermot. They were all small, all relatively non-threatening – the family had always survived.

Each time they moved, they moved on to another welfare file and another police file, bringing their innocuous catalogue of inadequacy along with them – an unemployed husband who drinks, a wife who took small overdoses of valium, children who attended special schools, a barring order against Jamesy, a small succession of dodgy welfare claims which were found out, a weekly appeal for Supplementary Welfare from the local Health Centre – just another poor family in a country where one-third of the population is living on the poverty line.

It was not expected that Mary would actually die under the burden of it all. The Church of the Immaculate Heart of Mary, where eight priests concelebrated Mass over the dead bodies of Mary Norris and her daughters Catherine, Sabrina, Fiona and Deirdre, and consoled her neighbours with the announcement that all five of God's adopted daughters had surely entered Heaven, is placarded with appeals to look for help before it is too late.

The placards, stretching from floor to ceiling of the church, capture the problems of, and pitiful end-of-the-line resources available to, those members of the working-class who have been brought to their knees by deprivation. Like advertising hoardings, they proclaim that Talbot House is there to help drug addicts, Madonna House is a holding centre for children in need of care, Stewart's Hospital school will attend to slow learners of any age, a senior citizen block of flats will cater for the abandoned elderly, and CURA will help those with troubled pregnancies.

One placard announces that the Little Sisters of the Assumption have moved into Clondalkin. Their house is ten yards away from the one where Mary lived. Among the objectives of the nuns, the placard firmly declares, is the development of women. The Sisters believe that women hold the key to the regeneration of the area, and hold the fort against doom.

Mary used some of the resources advertised by the Church and devised many of her own. Her life was a catalogue of hard work, its sole end the procurement of the one thing that she could understand very well, which was money. Much of that went to Jamesy, and the rest on rent, fuel and food for the children. For herself, she demanded only cigarettes. The things that money could not buy, such as parenting skills, affection, literacy and financial management were beyond her reach.

A community worker recalls talking with Mary about food. She suggested that instead of tinned steak and kidney pie and bottles of lemonade, Mary should shop for other things. The community worker offered to accompany Mary to the supermarket to do the week's shopping.

Mary agreed then took to her bed, saying she couldn't face it. The worker spent Mary's money for her, bringing back a bag of potatoes, mince, eggs and vegetables. "Look, Mary, that will keep you for a week." Two days later, Mary landed round in the welfare office to cadge some supplementary benefit.

"The kids don't like that kind of food. I have to buy the old stuff," she said. The nuns enrolled Mary in their house-keeping classes. One of Mary's closest friends, who marvels now at how much she herself managed to save, and how her children's health improved, through what she learned from the nuns, remembers Mary's attendance at the kitchen-school.

"She loved being among the women. She kept us all in stitches with her jokes and her stories. She disrupted us entirely, then she dropped out. She said she preferred to eat tinned foods."

Mary grew on people. The friend explained how neighbours constantly rallied to the woman who was always troubled. A lawyer whom Mary visited in the Law Library every fortnight remembers the first time he met her, in 1973. He worked then with the Free Legal Aid Company, a group of voluntary legal students who helped people decode the welfare maze.

"Our office was in the Vincent de Paul building in the inner city. She hoped her poor health would get her extra points, and persuaded the Corpo to transfer the family out of a slum flat. Her marriage had only started. It was in trouble. She was tiny, and thin, and had a quirky humour. I took to her."

Some time later, the lawyer came across Mary begging at the entrance to the Hibernian Hotel. He chatted with her, gave her money, and resumed the relationship. "She'd come down to the Law Library once a fortnight, send for me, and I'd give her a cheque or cash. She always carried a letter I gave her authorising her to cash the cheque at my bank on the Green. Towards the end, we didn't talk much. She'd tell her stories, I'd half listen. She'd receive her money, which is really all she came in for."

Neighbours know the lawyer's name, but don't know the name of another benefactor, who saw to it that Mary's ESB bills were presented to a certain bank and paid by that bank. Mary's excellent status with the ESB ensured that shortly before the fire in June she was able to buy a ghetto-blaster in credit from them.

Speaking amid the ashes of the June fire, Mary pointed to the transistor and said she had bought it for Catherine, to help the girl forget the fire that had engulfed Mary's mother's house. Catherine had been staying with her granny in Ballyfermot, when a blaze killed the granny and Catherine's uncle.

The gardai are satisfied that the fire had nothing to do with the fires that regularly broke out in Mary's own homes. The death of her mother and brother was a separate end to a separate catalogue of disasters that had characterised Mary's pre-marriage life – one brother serving life in England, another serving fifteen years in Mountjoy, a third killed in Ballyfermot during gang warfare between petty thieves.

Mary's mother was of travelling people stock, who married and settled down with a local man. Her friends remember Mary at fifteen selling paper roses in Ballyfermot. By sixteen she was pregnant, then married.

She stayed close to her parents, regularly going to chat with them. She would see her mother several times a week. After her mother burned to death on April 16, Mary was plunged into grief. An intimate conversational outlet had been destroyed. "She loved to talk. She came down here every Monday looking for money, but you knew perfectly well that she really wanted a conversation. She was lonely," says a member of the Rowlagh Health Centre.

She always brought some of her children with her. Sometimes she left them behind in the Health Centre, saying she wanted them taken into care, and she often brought them to hospital saying the same thing, but then she frequently adopted a similar attitude to Jamesy.

One day she wanted to rid of him, the next she wanted to stay with him. After a few hours in the Health Centre, the social worker would bring the children back to Mary's house, a few steps away. Mary would ask if the children had been given their dinner, and if they had, she would grin with delight. She had seen to it that her children were fed, one way or another, another small victory to chalk up against the failure of her mothering skills, which the cot death of her baby Shirley, years ago, seemed to represent to her.

She took her own steps against Jamesy, obtaining a court order barring him from the house on the grounds of assault. He wandered on back home anyway. Sometimes, when it got too much, she telephoned the guards from a neighbour's house. She informed them anonymously that it would be worth their while to check the Norris home for stolen goods. They might lift Jamesy and take him away for a while, she explained to her neighbour. This scheme backfired once when the guards removed the family television set, a massive brand new thing.

It took her days, with receipt and a completely accurate description of the shop where she bought it, to get it back.

There was one seeming scam, which preceded the three fires this year in Liscarne Gardens, which was not her fault, the neighbours swear. Mary had arranged years ago that social welfare payments be made out separately for her and Jamesy. He got £36 a week for himself; she got £74.35 for herself and the six children. Because she was illiterate, the neighbours filled out the necessary forms for her, every year, declaring the circumstances.

The separate payments were understood by the Corporation to indicate that Jamesy did not live with her, and her rent was adjusted to fifty pence a week. Then last October, when the new four-bedroomed houses went up, a neighbour suggested that Mary apply for one. It was near, she'd still have the company of friends she had built up, and there'd be more room for the couple, the four growing daughters and the two sons.

The neighbours helped her fill out the form. Someone in the Corpo noticed that the form showed that Jamesy lived with her, despite the separate payments, and an official landed round to announce that Mary's rent would go up to £15 a week, including back payments. That was a massive sum out of her £74, and a dreadful punishment, the neighbours felt, given that Mary had never handled the forms and had been truthful.

It meant that Mary had to work even harder to supply her family's needs. Shortly after that, the first fire occurred, then the one that might justify a newspaper plea for re-housing, then the one that killed Mary and the four girls. Re-housing might have meant new forms, and a Corpo official who was not entirely alert, and perhaps a restoration of low rent to Mary and Jamesy - these are the things neighbours wonder about as they look back over Mary's life and scams, and Jamesy's peripatetic life around the Corporation houses of Dublin.

Mary's hard work included petty shop-lifting. The judges always let her go after hearing her stories. The last conviction, she told me, was for stealing a pair of black slacks which she needed to wear to her mother's funeral. Under gentle nudging of her memory by a neighbour, Mary realised that she had stolen the trousers before her mother's death.

That she needed clothes, there is no doubt. Her money always went on the others, particularly to Jamesy. Sometimes when the women decided to go to Finche's for a celebration of their own, Mary would wear Catherine's Confirmation outfit.

She was so thin and small, the child's clothes fitted her perfectly.

She was so thin that the Health Centre allowed a special payment of £10 a week for a dietary supplement for her alone. It was not felt, however, that she would spend the money on herself. An arrangement was made with a supermarket that the cheque supplied to Jamesy would be spent only on good food for Mary.

Jamesy had been used to making his own arrangements for what he considered were his and Mary's needs in Finche's pub. He asked there that she not be allowed in before ten o'clock at night, after the children were safely in bed, and then only if he were in the pub himself. In the last week of Mary's life, Jamesy's request was made redundant.

Mary was barred by management from going in there without, him around, because in the days before her death she had taken to going round the pub collecting money to replace the furniture damaged in the June fire. She concentrated on customers whom, she deluded herself, did not know her. Mary was tirelessly and anonymously organising a benefit collection for her own family. It was foolish but it was funny, and neighbours cheered her ingenuity.

She didn't often go to Finche's, but when she did she amused her friends by her antics in getting round Jamesy's pub-decree. She would drop to her hands and knees and secure a table out of his sight. The Finche's is a vast, darkened place, with two small windows paying perfunctory lip-service to the world beyond the public bar. Under it's electric light, and with the television flickering steadily in the background, it is impossible to tell day from night.

Men who have not been able to get work, to whom day and night are as one long nightmare, crowd into it from the moment it opens. There are no self-help classes for the unemployed men of Clondalkin. The meagre voluntary and state resources are aimed at women who keep the family's body and soul together.

The men who do stay at home get under their women's feet. There is unconcealed irritation at the traditionally unnatural crowding together, during working hours, of a husband and wife and adult children as well, in a house where there is no hope that jobs will one day come.

Living on the edges of society, Mary had no hope, but a gift for cheering other women up. She would suggest an evening in the pub, and then, as one of her friends put it, "I will never forget what she did for me. All my life I only ever had birthday cards from my family - from brothers and sisters, and parents and my husband. One night in the pub, the lights went out, and a barman appeared with a cake lit with candles, and Mary started singing Happy Birthday. She had arranged the whole thing. She took me out of my world, do you know what I mean, and brought me into a public one. For the first time in my life, other people knew it was the anniversary of the day I was born."

None of the women for whom she arranged these treats minded at all when Mary called around next day and borrowed money to keep her going. She was scrupulously careful to repay her debts to her neighbours, in feast and famine. She often lent them money herself.

Her children sensed that begging and repaying was a way of communication. The night of the final fire, Fiona and Deirdre had gone up and down the road borrowing tea bags. A neighbour decided to call in and see if Mary was in a food-crisis. There were plenty of tea bags and need of none. The children's allowance money had been paid out only that day, and Jamesy had given her some of it.

Mary and the neighbour burst out laughing, and went on to celebrate Mary's latest stroke of luck – the suite which had replaced the one burned in June, thanks to donations from the Gay Byrne Show and a welfare supplement, was installed in the repaired livingroom, and only that night a second suite had been delivered to Mary's door.

The neighbour did not question its provenance, because Mary had so many stories to explain things. Instead, she sat in this second suite in the kitchen, marvelling at it. It might or might not, she knew, be sold out the back door, as Mary was often wont to do when a deluge of luck came her way.

The kitchen suite, where before there had only been a humble table and chair, added to the kitchen fire and smoke that killed Mary and her daughters hours later as they slept.

Mary, modest in the extreme, had worried about her daughters. When she discovered Catherine bleeding before the age of ten, she consulted the other women about the early arrival of menstruation. The women spoke with Catherine, and Catherine talked of a man in a van who had offered her lollipops, and touched her. There had been no menstruation. The neighbours advised Mary to take Catherine to hospital. Mary said later that one hospital talked of sexual interference, another had dismissed the notion. The gardai are checking out Mary's story now.

They have also interviewed the neighbour to whom Mary turned last year when she thought that a strange smell and substance seeped from Fiona's little genital area.

This neighbour looked at Fiona, then aged six, and said her genitals were raw and distorted and swollen, and bore no visible relationship to the rawness that occurs regularly in little children who wet their pants, or are not regularly bathed. In any case, Mary kept a spotless house, and turned her children out beautifully.

The neighbour advised hospital again. The gardai are checking hospital records. Neighbours, drawing on their deepest, most affectionate resources, could not adequately cope with Mary's worries about her two girls. The Church has no placard drawing attention to this latest crisis of which Ireland is becoming painfully aware.

A community worker to whom Mary sent Catherine for sex education wonders in retrospect, now, if Mary was sending out yet another signal for help. So many signals, so many small signals, so many conflicting stories from Mary, who did the very best she could, scrabbling for money for her family, while living an outwardly laughing life of the deepest loneliness and despair. She married young, she died young, she never had the leisure or opportunity to grow up. Since becoming a child-bride, she was pre-occupied with being a mother.

It's hard enough being a mother, if you know how to be, and have a partner who knows how to be a father, and both have the time and maturity and freedom from financial woe to

acquire the skills. Love is not always sufficient, although among the very poorest love is all they have to offer.

Social workers are reluctant in the extreme to remove children from their parents, especially given the miserly alternative in this country to a family home. In the vast area where Mary lived, in any case, called Area Five in Eastern Health Board parlance, cut-backs have reduced the number of social workers from five to one solitary overworked individual. This person had not the time to call on Mary between the second fire and the third one which killed her.

A voluntary worker, who discussed the plight of the Norris family after Mary had spoken with me, offered a consolation born out of experience in an area deluged with deprivation. "Children can survive anything," she said.

The four Norris girls did not.

For Catherine (12), Sabrina (8), Fiona (7) and Deirdre (3), there was no more salvation than there was for Mary, their mother.

In 1988, Mary's husband, James, was convicted of her murder.

TALLAGHT I
Kieran Fagan

"And where's your nephew going to live?", Mrs Palin asked pointedly, knowing full well that if it had been Dalkey or Killiney she would never have heard the end of it.

"Tallaght", replied my aunt, a bit doubtfully. Then she attempted a recovery. "The purchase houses, of course." But it was too late. Mrs Palin's sniff said it all.

On and off over the past 20 years that sniff has recurred whenever Tallaght was mentioned. It took different forms. "Tallaght is the last refuge of the pass Leaving Certificate", said some. "What do you call a Tallaght man in a suit?", others asked. "The accused."

Many Tallaght residents are Dublin people first and Tallaght people second. A good number emigrated on leaving school, then returned to Ireland in the aftermath of Sean Lemass's briefly rising tide, and were promptly hit by the collapse in industrial jobs which followed the EC membership in the 1970s. Even today some of the new generation of Tallaght's young adults have English and Scottish accents. The irony is that they can find themselves re-emigrating to the country where they were born during their parents' exile from Ireland.

Tallaght was to be a new town, we were told. Part of the planner Myles Wright's blueprint to "house" the population explosion in south and west Dublin. Note the verb "house". This is where Mrs Palin's sniff began, and it has continued in one form or another, right up to this day. Everyone needs somewhere to live, but no one wants to feel they are being sent to a reservation. My family is fairly representative. We got a mortgage on a small well-built terraced house in an estate of 300 on the outskirts of Tallaght village in 1973. Then the explosion, which was to take the population from less than 1,000 in the 1950s to 80,000 in the 1980s, was really underway.

Fiona was then eight. Sally was born in 1975. In our little cul-de-sac of nineteen houses, six girls were born within twelve months of each other. If I am still around in the year 2000 I hope to write a "where are they now?" piece about the lives of Miriam Dooley, Sandra Groome, Vanessa Flood, Caroline Carey, Deborah O'Connor and Sally Fagan.

In Tallaght things happened at incredible speed. McKone builders were completing new houses in Millbrook Lawns at the rate of five and six a day. A tiler working in the Springfield estate told me that he was called down from rooftops three times in one week to drive pregnant women to give birth in the Coombe Hospital. Four new primary schools were opened on the same day.

There seemed to be a pattern. Houses first, then, if you were lucky, roads, followed fairly smartly by a church and school. There was a great flowering of residents and tenants associations which fought stoutly against builders, the local authorities (we were blessed with two, Dublin Corporation and Dublin County Council), - and - with greatest relish of all - amongst themselves.

Who now remembers the "Battle of Bolbrook Lodge", over which two adjoining estates fought a mighty war? The council offered the house as a community centre, but neither estate could tolerate the other having access. The community centre idea was dropped and honour was satisfied. The other crowd never set foot in it. But one way and another, estate by estate, teething problems were resolved. Schools, health centres, parks, libraries were slowly but surely put into place. Despite the fact that this was the fastest growing urban area in Europe, or so we were told, a process of normalisation was moving across Tallaght, from the areas which had been developed first.

This process was sufficiently slow for there always to be something for the Mrs Palins of this world to sniff at. Then a number of latent problems came to a head around the same time. Many Tallaght residents came from fairly tight-knit communities which had been very good at resolving their own problems. The extended family structure which meant that

132

children and young married couples alike were "minded" by a network of older family and friends was shattered by the move to a new housing estate, miles away from the rest of the clan.

No longer would Uncle Billy spot Our Kevin thieving apples, and give him a swift box, and that would be the end of that. A grandfather was not on hand to notice that Mary's eldest lad was going a bit wild, and find some way of diverting his energies. Then local authority tenants were offered up to £5,000 to relinquish their tenancies, in a well-meant but socially disastrous attempt to stimulate housebuilding. There was an immediate exodus of the more settled families "trading up", and some of the precious newly-formed "social cement" was chipped away.

The bloke who always organised the football or boxing club, the older woman who was on hand to advise her younger "sisters" with family problems moved on, and the process of replacing the extended family was delayed.

This coincided with the first wave of new Tallaght adolescents. A minority of these got out of control and took to the dangerously attractive macho "sport" of car stealing. One celebrated case made national news, and has become the stuff of Greek tragedy, damaging the lives of the victim, Eamonn Gavin, and the accused Joseph Grogan and Joseph Meleady, and all their families.

Our Fiona went to school with the two youths. The day after they were arrested she told me that they had not done it, and was able to give me the name of the "real" driver of the stolen car. "Everybody in school knows they didn't do it", she said. That proves nothing except the fact that their guilt was disputed from the very beginning. In another incredible twist, a youth who confessed to being in the stolen car was jailed for perjury.

My own view is that the car owner made an honest mistake in identifying the thieves as Grogan and Meleady. He has paid dearly for being involved in something in which he had no choice. They have paid an even higher price, a five year jail sentence apiece.

The identification of car thieves as the "Tallaght Two" did not do much for the image of the young people of Ireland's third largest centre of population.

In fact it brought down on our heads the attention of the "chattering classes". These are well-meaning people, who like the late Eamon de Valera only have to look into their own hearts to know what is good for the people of Ireland. They write newspaper columns, appear on TV, and in the course of time become famous for being famous.

It was inevitable that the shining light of their wisdom would be beamed on Tallaght. The first analysis was: lack of facilities. I was never quite sure what facilities were. There's a swimming pool, a bowling alley, two libraries and five bus routes within ten minutes walk from my house. Would, for example, the additional provision of an ice rink deter some little gouger from trying to steal my car?

The second analysis rested on slightly more solid ground - the lack of a town centre. All would be well when Tallaght got its town centre. There would be a town hall where folk could gather and engage in communal, none-too-taxing activities, proper to their Lada-owning status. And an office where they could pay their differential rents, or whatever it is they do. And a bank in which to cash their social welfare cheques. Perhaps even a sports goods shop, track suits for the purchase of...

None of these earnest thinkers on social issues ever bent their minds to the futility of trying to construct a self-contained new town six or seven miles from an expanding capital city. Of course it would be helpful if Dublin County Council could emerge from its bunker in downtown Dublin and set up shop where it is accessible to the punters. And Dublin Corporation, a major landowner in the area, has no means of being made accountable to the people of Tallaght for its actions there.

But this is not the stuff of great columns or searing TV documentaries, pithy, passionate and committed, about the deprivations suffered by unfortunates living "out in Tallaght". You need something more dramatic to justify headlines like

134

"suburban sprawl without a soul". (Sprawl is a word subject to regional variations. What is "spacious" in south Dublin "Dortland" becomes sprawl five miles to the west.)

But were they grateful, these humble helots, for the searing expose of their miserable conditions? Were they what?

Immediately after publication, a tide of rank ingratitude breaks on the head of the committed columnist who had addressed the problems of the downtrodden. First manifestation is the summons from an editor or a TV executive, throwing a very pronounced "wobbly". He (it is usually but not always a he) finds there are 80,000 people out there, living perfectly normal lives, all giving out socks to him about the way they have been depicted.

"They do not eat their young, ride around on the bonnet of their own cars, drink cider from plastic containers while sitting at the roadside, or exhibit other forms of irrational behaviour which you Ms Concerned Columnist ascribe to them.

"The phones haven't stopped ringing – I thought they weren't supposed to have phones out there. The bloody fax machine is spewing out yards of abuse. Look, we'd better send X, tell him to find something positive and get some pretty pictures, like now, immediately, we'll run it on Monday. Not one word of criticism, right?"

(If the offending item had been on RTE, harassed executive would be be arranging for two or three Tallaght old folk, with their teeth in, all the better to look happy and positive with, to appear on Live at Three, pronto.)

Either way the corrective message would be put across. Tallaght is not as bad as all that. These people are not the poor and dishonest (through no fault of their own) tribe we said they were. (Real moral of story: no media organisation can afford to alienate a country's third largest centre of population, even if they were cannibals.)

Which, of course, they are not. In fact they are infused with something which more than compensates for their unhealthy junk food diets. THEY ARE FILLED WITH COMMUNITY SPIRIT.

Of all the insults visited on the long-suffering people of south west Dublin, this has to be the worst. To be covered with this syrupy confection, this sticky fictional goo laid all over our downtrodden lives, just because A Great Thinker got it wrong first time around, is more than flesh and blood should have to bear.

Just like the rest of the world, and in very similar proportions, Tallaght is composed of those who help themselves, those who help others, and those who need help.

Labour TD Mervyn Taylor spoke for all of us when he said "We welcome sensible discussion of problems which arise in Tallaght. What we object to is discussion of Tallaght as if it were the problem."

A study carried out by Irish Marketing Surveys or the developers of the £85 million shopping centre known as The Square showed that in terms of patterns of consumption, Tallaght was not noticeably different from the rest of Dublin. The number of skilled workers was slightly higher than the citywide norm: otherwise the breakdown of social classes was much the same as the city at large. In fact we are all we ever wanted to be, the same as anybody else.

There's another wave of development getting underway, and another inflow of new Tallaght residents will have their own story to tell. The experience of some of the people of west Tallaght, the most recent arrivals, differs in detail from that of a previous wave to which I belong. But the overall experience of jigsaw development, with frustrating waits where some pieces are not fitted in as quickly as they should, is common to all. The biggest gap, The Square, has now been filled. Having what looks like the best shopping centre in Ireland, here in Tallaght has done more than provide 1500 jobs. It has given morale a badly-needed lift. It has also shifted the local centre of gravity to a point between east and west Tallaght, equidistant, in terms of time not kilometres, from Dublin city and Blessington in west Wicklow.

The Regional Technical College, opening in 1992, will alter the social mix again. It may be that a new generation will have a different view of Tallaght as an independent entity, with a former capital of Ireland, Dublin, as its near neighbour.

My ambition for Tallaght is a more modest one. I am hoping for a small, not too crowded, public house. A quirk of the laws means a dearth of licences, so our pubs tend to be vast barns. Every sraidbhaile in Ireland has 75 pubs, it seems, but we have only a handful. It is not true that a pilot of an Air Corps jet, while attempting to land at nearby Baldonnel, mistook the lights in the carpark of the Belgard Inn for the runway, and landed safely in the front lounge. It isn't true, but it could be.

If you see a drunk in a Dublin city pub, with a pint in one hand and a bus guide in the other, how do you sober him up? Tell him the last bus to Tallaght has gone.

We'd be better off with a sprinkling of small neighbourhood public houses, true "locals" like The Rover's Return. Imagine how that idea would galvanise the residents' associations...

And now having lived here longer than I have lived anywhere else, I'm inclined to think that I shall stay. My last journey will probably be to the quiet graveyard adjoining St. Maelruan's Anglican church, where I hope they will find room for me in the shade of a tree. The problem is that it, like the rest of Tallaght, is filling up fast.

TALLAGHT II
Leland Bardwell

I went to live in Killinarden in 1980 having been evicted from a house we rented in a lane at the back of Leeson Street.

There was a touch of rain that eviction day - cold for July. Our furniture was out on the street. The Sheriff leant against his Honda 50, a small unsmiling man.

"I have a Court Order against you and your husband."

"I have no husband."

"But it is for you and your husband."

"I have three sons but no husband."

"I have a Court Order for you and your husband to vacate the premises on this day."

"I know."

He scratched his head under his helmet. I said I could go back inside and make him a cup of tea. He declined.

We stood, leaning on bits of furniture. A light rain began to fall.

The Corpo, after six months of intense argument had agreed to rehouse us in Tallaght. We didn't want to go to Tallaght. Tallaght was out in the Styx. My sons were still at school in Dublin.

"It's Tallaght or nowhere," they had said.

My sons had musical instruments. They were getting wet.

The Sheriff looked around as though he might find a husband for me somewhere.

"It is very irregular," he said.

"I know."

I looked back at the little house we had lived happily in for eleven years. It seemed stretched and hollow without us. It wasn't our place any more, it was different.

The Sheriff took the key I gave him. He put it in his pocket.

He rode off into the drizzle on his Honda 50.

I quote from an article I wrote at the time: "We have been housed in a brand new house in a recently built housing estate in Killinarden at the foothills of the Dublin mountains, about three miles the far side of the old village of Tallaght. From our front window we have a fine view of the hills, a sweep of colour and freshness: there is little or no traffic pollution. There is a line of shops - a mini-market, a hardware shop, a hairdressers, a bookies and a Chinese Take-away. There is also a pub. The houses, sub-contracted by the Corpo, are jerry-built with paper-thin party walls.

"There is a patch of land some thirty feet by eighteen behind the house and a small front patch as well. This back patch, which I am attacking in order to make a garden, I find lacking in top-soil. For some unknown reason the builders have removed this soil and with tyrannical sadism strewn the garden with concrete blocks. Water runs down from the hills and gathers in little gulches. The clay is thick and heavy.

"The estate is a mile from the Blessington Road. There is no foot path on this stretch and half-way along it stands a telephone kiosk, faceless, an abandoned skeleton in the ever-present wind.

"The pub is like a border check-point, surrounded by hoardings and barbed wire. No one under twenty five is allowed to enter its doors. My immediate neighbours, victims of the recent city clearances like ourselves, are needle-thin women, with already two or three babies and husbands on the labour. I constantly hear the cry *Don't touch them, thems your mammies pills*. The toddlers play out in the wide street amongst the detritus left by the builders, abandoned cranes and earth-removers, rusting in the mud."

Poverty was endemic. The mini-market was empty except on dole-day; the till-girl, bored from lack of work, frequently absent from the till. Coming up to Christmas the young mothers would come in to put another pound down on some shoddy expensive toy which they hoped to get for their children. These young mothers were cut off from their families

140

and their only recourse was to walk the long mile with go-cart and toddlers to the Blessington Road in the hopes that they might eventually get a bus to take them back to the city for the day to see their own mothers. The unreliable bus, when it eventually came, was usually full up which meant endless waits on this dangerous road.

Above and beyond these almost insurmountable difficulties, no phones, few buses, no street life, no late-night hucksters, no friends from childhood, of which the planners of these estates are valiantly oblivious, there is something yet more insidious that eats into your soul. One becomes increasingly aware that one has allowed oneself to be manipulated by "those men out there", whose aims to destroy everything most dear to urban people, have been elevated to fundamental principles. Myself, I became a prey to fantasies, unable to work. I spent hours pouring over house-ads and transfer columns in the hope that something would come to my aid in a magical fashion. For my sons it was worse. Cut off from their companions of school and college, to continue their education they had to cycle the twelve hilly miles in and out of Dublin in all weathers. One by one, they left.

As the neighbouring children ran out to the first few bars of the *Skaters Waltz* blaring from the ice cream van we knew there was no way of solving the larger issues of the day no more than would these kids with their hot coppers in their hands.

In contrast to us, "respectable" prisoners of poverty, the itinerants, camped beyond the yellow polluted stream, with their bangers and their horses seemed to have an enviable air of freedom and survival in spite of their atrocious living conditions.

What is this place called Tallaght now? The name, roughly translated, means The Land of the Plague. There used to be a monastery there, which presumably tried to succour the dying. A mere thirty years ago, the old village, built on a rise, well above the soggy foothills, consisted of a solitary street. It was a "pretty" village, marginally forgotten. Then when the city clearances began in the sixties and seventies and Ballymun was deemed a failure the planners hit on the notion that the last available tracts of land outside the city that no rich people had pounced on were in or near Tallaght or Clondalkin.

Gradually the new housing estates near the old village were extended further and further out off the Blessington Road. So Tallaght, as most city people believe, is not a great homogenous whole. The outlying estates of Killinarden Fetercairn and Jobstown are separate entities. When people read in the papers about the wonderful new shopping emporium that went up last year they imagine it is a centre of happiness for the entire population. The irony of this is obvious.

The new generation living in the estates near this centre has indeed made valiant strides to structure its own society with music and drama centres, adult education – the women especially attending new courses, having established their own creche; but there is still a shortage of local jobs, and worse, as yet no hospital to cater for a population the size of Limerick. But the three or four estates I've mentioned are forgotten; they are not Tallaght, never were Tallaght, and the residents there will remain bewildered and downtrodden while the great capitalist machine continues its policy of hiding what it can't come to terms with thereby creating its own ghettos as in any third world country.

TALLAGHT III
Heather Brett

I've been living in Tallaght the last three and a half years and
the first two things that struck me about the place was that,
one, it was dirty, and two, my mother wouldn't like it.
Nobody could call Tallaght a pretty village, it is dirty looking,
always somehow to be in that perpetual state of "being
improved", various road works and construction are as much a
part of the scenery as the large areas of wasteland between its
numerous housing estates. Even I can't call Tallaght pretty, but
I do like it, I like living here and although I think generally
people want Tallaght improved a bit, I doubt if it'll make a lot
of difference.

Tallaght is some seven or eight miles from Dublin, south-
west, and although on a height it is nestled among some
beautiful countryside. Behind the infamous housing estates of
Killinarden and Jobstown lie the mountains of Seahan, Corrig
and Kippur. Tallaght is really only a stones throw from some
great picnicking areas and local beauty spots along the Dodder.
And the nicest thing about this is that the people of Tallaght
really go there. On fine Sundays the buses are crowded
towards the Blessington Lakes area, after all there's not a lot to
do in the village itself.

Although records of Tallaght go as far back as 2000 B.C.
there's not that much for the tourist, apart from the beautiful
priory and its famous walnut tree. The part I found interesting
was that the name Tallaght or Tamhlacht, means "Plague
Grave" so called because thousands of the first settlers died and
were interred here.

For me it's not the history of the place or even how it looks
that makes me like it - it's the people and I think Tallaght's got
some of the best. Tallaght is a community. Even though it has

despairing numbers of unemployed, the people here seem to weather it all very well. There's no lethargy here, everybody does something even it's only taking care of their houses or gardens. Tallaght people are friendly, and I should know, since it's not too long ago I came here a complete stranger. If there's an important issue, especially involving children, Tallaght people are the first to support it. In the marches over the education cuts Tallaght gave a worthy response.

The women are great here. They're into just about everything and the huge availability of classes for adults here proves it. Everybody's busy, from baking to knitting - writing to oil painting.

There are lots of teenagers here, droves of them and yes, there are the inevitable problems of crimes like burglary, car thefts, gang harassment, etc. and I know this sort of thing is on the increase here, but it wouldn't make me want to move - not yet anyway. I think the thing to do is be positive about Tallaght or anywhere one lives, for that matter. There are also quite a lot of travelling people here, less now though, than when I came here in '85, but for the most part they pose no big problem and things seem to be happy enough.

Some people here are a bit unhappy about the rise in crime rate and have thought of moving, but with the housing market the way it is it takes a long time to sell a house here or find a suitable one in a better area. On the whole Tallaght people like it here and will fight to keep their rights, hence the recent marked response in most Neighbourhood Watch Schemes. That's the dark side of living here, but doesn't everywhere have its problems?

If there's a good response to the Neighbourhood Watch Scheme, there's an even better response to summer projects that the community puts on. Street parties, field days, fairs, you name it and somewhere along the summer it'll happen. From kids to grannies participate always, the church likewise, and not, thankfully, in an overbearing manner. Communion and Confirmation times are just another excuse for neighbours to get together and have a good time. Having said this I don't mean one can't get "lost" here and be completely on their own, no-one bothers you unless you invite it. Personally I reckon it's a good as a place as any to live, if you're a family, it's family orientated, if your a loner, Tallaght will understand.

Having reread this I find I could be biased - after all, anywhere is better than the north, but actually I do think it's good here. However, a few months after I came here I did some poems about the place, rather sombre pieces looking back on it, but I think I was struck more by the somewhat desolate places than the life here then.

Anyhow - I'm staying.

TALLAGHT IV
Annette Halpin

We moved out to live in Tallaght in the Autumn of '73, a month before my third baby under three was born.

There are certain things in life we can never fully understand until we have experienced them ourselves. Moving out to Tallaght was one of these things for me.

I could never have imagined what it was like to feel so isolated, abandoned, lonely. To find myself confined without transport, without phones, without shops, without anywhere to go, not knowing anyone, alone.

My hardships really began the morning after I arrived, although 8 months pregnant, I had to walk two miles to the nearest shop and two miles back. As it came near the time of my delivery, I would begin to panic each night after the last bus had gone, because without phone or transport, I didn't know how I would get to the Rotunda hospital which was 10 miles away. The roads had no lights, and you'd never see a taxi.

But we were very hopeful. A new town would be built in two years, we were told, and the scenery was beautiful.

As there were no community centres or halls built within the housing estates it left women in a very vulnerable position, especially in winter time. There was nowhere people could meet each other, except knock on someone's door, but as people were strangers, it was hard to know who you could trust. Most of the women felt isolated and alone, some more than others, but because we were young and had no-one to talk to about it we thought there must be something wrong with us, and so we put on a brave face and covered it up.

I remember speaking to a woman one day who was smiling and looked the picture of happiness. The next day I heard she had been taken into St. Lomans, suffering from an overdose. This happened a lot. Most women survived the overdoses, unfortunately some didn't, and sadly this is still a fact of life in Tallaght today, so unbearable is the isolation and lack of facilities for some women.

But on the positive side, there are now hundreds of women working as volunteers in an effort to break down the isolation and build a better community, for as soon as women began sharing and opening up to each other, we began to realise there was nothing wrong with us, it was the situation we found ourselves in that was wrong.

A situation planned and brought about by people who would never have to live in Tallaght. People who had no empathy with us, who presumed, as one planner told me, "that everyone would have, if not two cars, then certainly one." People who would never know what it was like to have to walk the two miles down and back to the village, with small babies, and bags of messages in all kinds of weather. People who still can't see the urgency of 85,000 people for basic amenities and resources.

Because of the insensitivity of successive governments and government bodies in failing to provide these amenities, thousands of people in Tallaght have had to endure unbearable hardships and suffering. Isolation, unemployment and poverty left many families in permanent ill health and great need.

Before every election we would hear of all the wonderful things that were going to happen. After years of waiting, people became sick and tired of talk and promises, of research and analysis, of surveys and studies. Tallaght became as it was called "The Forgotten City".

What I and many others began to realise was that we could no longer depend on people who had no empathy with us to determine our future and development, all future plans for the development of Tallaght would have to start where the people were at, and respond to their needs. Like a tree grows from its roots participation by the people in the growth and development of their own area and community was essential.

One of the things which opened my eyes to the lack of empathy, was the Combat Poverty programme which was introduced in the mid eighties. This was the first real money that came into Tallaght. At that stage Tallaght women had been doing voluntary work for years. Indeed it was only with the ideas and efforts of local women that the project could have come about. Yet no Tallaght women were employed. Professional women were brought in from outside to articulate our local ideas, develop them and be paid for it. This put us back 20 years, instead of combating the poverty of women in Tallaght it actually impoverished us even more. We had at least been speaking for ourselves and our own needs, now others were speaking for us. I remember sitting in a room one day with eleven people all discussing the future of Tallaght, and I was the only one from Tallaght. It was crazy (for the first time I understood the term EEC mercenaries). Community development to some professionals is fine it seems once it is controlled, once locals don't lose the run of themselves, and start thinking that they are equal, and worse, start applying for jobs at it. This approach shows a great lack of faith and empathy in the people on the ground. Had even half the money been put into locals and local groups so much more could have been accomplished.

Because of the neglect and disillusionment of the first few years Tallaght people began to come together with creative ideas to look at the needs, to look at the potential. The results were unbelievable. Centres and groups began to spring up out of the community to serve the needs of the people, to bring about development, to improve the quality of life. There are now hundreds of groups and dozens of centres in Tallaght, the majority founded and run by Tallaght people on a voluntary basis.

The interesting thing about these groups is that although they have been set up in different parts of Tallaght, by different people at different times, to cater for a wide variety of needs, the same spirit and ethos seems to run through all of them. I.E.

1. Their service is unconditional.

149

2. They are non party political and non denominational.

3. They have a high degree of skill and caring.

4. There is equality of treatment and opportunity for all who use the service, no matter what their financial position may be.

They include a wide variety of self help and support groups. Centres and groups dealing with alternative and preventive health care and medicine, with creativity and awareness, with education and development, with healing and counselling, with information and rights, with community unemployment, poverty and isolation issues.

Most of these groups have no government funding, in fact I doubt if the government is even aware that half of them exist.

Although we at last have "The Square" we still have no leisure centre, we have no hospital or emergency centre, we have no third level college as yet. We have a huge youth population, and high unemployment with very little job prospects.

I have seen children with cuts that really needed stitching, but because of the distance, and because of the bus fare, mothers have had to put a bandage on and hope for the best. I have seen pregnant women collapse and faint while waiting for a bus to and from maternity hospitals. I have seen the emergence of what could have been serious gang warfare, because of the poverty and unemployment.

Given the odds that were against us, we should now be in dire straits, but there is a great spirit in Tallaght and people always manage to look at the funny side. They are quick to observe characters, and yet be understanding of them, such as conscientious objecters who object to everything and contribute to nothing. Moanalizas who always look at the negative side. Do-it-yourself fanatics (who could make an arse for a cat) and snobs who pretend that they live anywhere else but Tallaght. One confused old woman said to me "For eighty years I thought I lived in Tallaght, but now they tell me I live in Templeogue".

If I were to write an account of my 17 years in Tallaght it would take a book not an essay, and maybe someday I will get around to writing a book. I believe the future of Tallaght lies with its people. Community for me now means living in common with the people around me.

Sharing the same transport system, breathing the same air, not always agreeing, feeling the same classism and oppression, hating the same inequalities and injustices, sharing the laughter the joy the humour, seeing the good days and the bad days. Living in common 24 hours of the day 365 days in the year.

Physically, socially, recreationally, emotionally, feeling the heartache at seeing the kids emigrate, when you know they have the potential, but have to leave the shagging country to realise it. Feeling the anger at seeing them exploited in part time employment with low wages. Feeling the despair at seeing them going on the Labour. Feeling the hopelessness and powerlessness at seeing the circle repeated. Wondering sometimes if the years of words and actions have made one bit of difference, knowing that they have. Living in common, listening to people talking and asking why.

Why should our kids have to emigrate? Why are they nearly all working below their potential?

Why has the Department of Labour allowed a situation to arise where thousands of part time workers are denied their rights, and middle men make big money?

Why are courses run by FAS not equiping people for employment? Why, after a six month course, are people told, "it's not enough", why not give them more?

Why are one or two groups getting huge funding and the rest getting none?

Why have the projects not gone back to the community when we were told they would?

Why are women discriminated against under the Social Employment Scheme?

Why has the Post Office been closed when everyone wants it left open, and the elderly need it?

Why are people who are not living in common, continually talking about their perception of our need, and making decisions about our lives?

Living in common. Seeing the joy, the support, the kindness people give each other.

Seeing the beauty of our children growing up.

Seeing the courage of men and women in their struggle.

Seeing the wisdom of the elderly and people getting on a bit in years, the smoothing of rough edges.

Seeing the celebration of life and love by the people of Tallaght, sharing it, living in common.

Sometimes I find myself moaning, when I'm all set for a good night out, and the bus, usually the 76, doesn't come. O not for me the easy life, I say. Not for me the comforts of a car, I've never had it easy, I've always had to rough it, and aren't you the stronger woman for it says himself, and when the revolution comes, you'll be ready.

THE GREAT SHAMROCK ROVERS REVIVAL

Eamon Dunphy

In April, 1984 Eamon Dunphy wrote the following article on Shamrock Rovers and Milltown for Magill Magazine. *It is reproduced here with a new epilogue.*

Rovers is a city institution. In the language of the street nobody says Shamrock Rovers, that's unnecessary. When you mention Rovers all kinds of images spring to mind: power, grandeur, style, success, excitement, crowds, in fact everything that League of Ireland football - Famous Chicken Football - does not possess.

The images evoked belong to the past. Which past depends on who you were talking to. Old men remember Rovers in the 20s and 30s. They recall the packed trams, John Joe Flood, Fulham and Fagan. Somewhat younger men remember Paddy Moore, Peter Farrell, the war years, rations and Rovers.

A younger generation still, my generation, which grew up in the 50s and early 60s remember the Rovers of Paddy Coad. Coad was a genius. He was a great inside forward - delicate, powerful, imaginative.

To a city of young men obsessed with soccer he was the best player we had ever seen. We knew that great football was played in England and further afield in mysterious places like Brazil. We had photos and cigarette cards with heroic yet distant names written on them. But we had no television. We had never actually seen the greats.

Occasionally you would meet The Boy Who'd Been to England, who'd seen Tom Finney play. This boy was envied in much the same way as later you would envy The Man Who Always Got The Pretty Girl.

For those of us who had never travelled in the pre-television age Paddy Coad and his Rovers team were It. The game they played was a game you grew up loving, their tricks, great feats and mannerisms were what you aspired to...Even if, as in my case, you didn't follow them, even if, as was true of those of us who didn't follow, you loathed them. You still knew that they were the best.

In the colourless tight-arsed city of that time Rovers represented romance and, if you longed to see them beaten, drama, as you waited with small clenched fists to see it happen.

The Rovers team was awesome. So deeply did they penetrate soul and imagination that now, twenty-five years on, I can tell you the team without reference to notes and there are hundreds and thousands out there who could chant along with me: O'Callaghan, Bourke, Mackey, Nolan, Keogh, Hennessey, McCann, Peyton, Ambrose, Coad, and Tuohy. Later on Tommy Hamilton sometimes played when Coad packed up.

Those legendary men won everything, if you wanted to see them you would have to have an early Sunday lunch, then to College Green where a vast anxious crowd would throng to await CIE's Football Specials. Many would walk from town on fine days and as your bus crawled along Appian Way and agonisingly slowly through Ranelagh the pavements were awash with hurrying people.

And so on up to Milltown Road to Glenmalure Park past dozens of hawkers selling apples, orr-emm-ges and chocolate. Rovers place in Irish football meant that they were the team to beat. For every other city team, especially my beloved Drums, and for every country team as well, the big day of the year was the day you played Rovers. They in their majesty were the yardstick by which we could measure our own heroes and thus our own small selves.

Thinking of it now takes the breath away from my cynical thirty-eight year old body. It was so beautiful.

The decline of League of Ireland football began when that team aged and died. Television, motor cars, and Sunday lunches in hotels you can blame - if blame you should - all those things for ending an era of sporting romance. But the link between the demise of Rovers and a bleak age in League of Ireland football is undeniable if not indeed denied.

The Rovers of the early 60s that won the FAI cup six years running was The Last Great Team. Thus, through the wretched twenty years decline of the game in this country it has been an article of faith among those who care about such things that "Irish football will never prosper, will never live again until Shamrock Rovers are great again".

That seductive theory is about to be put to the test. The resurrection of The Hoops is under way at last. Rovers last won the league in 1964. Now with a handful of games to go they are clear at the top of the table and look uncatchable.

They are back not just winning but winning in the old way, stylishly, powerfully, grandly. For the past few months, the old images have drifted nostalgically by. The Great Shamrock Rovers Revival is important for two reasons. There is, as outlined above, the not insignificant nostalgic glow of times that are now gone forever. More relevant to those who have dreams to dream today there is the hope that the rampant Rovers of '84 will breathe life into a domestic soccer team that is spiritually and financially out on its feet.

The game flourishes among the people here as it has never done before. As seen on television it inspires and attracts more people than it ever has. More people that is to *play* the game. Junior and Schoolboy soccer lures people in their tens of thousands out onto cold and wet public parks every winter weekend.

The return of John Giles to Millmount in 1977 encouraged the Kilcoyne family of building fame to invest real money in making Rovers great again. In playing terms they failed. Giles who had – and subsequently has – managed successfully around the world had a view of the game that was too sophisticated for part-time pros. He too, was attracted by the dream of making the past come back to life. He too had grown up in Dublin in the 50s. But there was never between him and the players he worked with at Milltown the unity of mind and

155

spirit you need to do the job.

Nevertheless, during those years, all the things that didn't happen elsewhere began to happen at Rovers. The ground was lovely, the pitch immaculate, the stands clean, the terraces neat. You could get a programme and a cup of tea, team changes were announced on a good public address system. Floodlights were acquired and good players who were paid decent wages...and every week!

And when none of this translated into playing success how the mean and shabby men laughed, or rather sniggered. "Doing it right...a lot of fucking good it's doing them". Thus the poisonous waft of triumphant mediocrity.

Giles departed slightly wounded from the war. This season Jim McLaughlin came. He had proved at Dundalk that he was the best manager in the league. Poorly paid, not really appreciated, minus resources that would be his at Rovers, Jim had won everything there was to win at Dundalk. A distinguished veteran of the English league class II he understood what Giles did not: how to play the game the part- time way.

His inspired personal touch has transformed players like Alan Campbell, Neville Steedman, John Cody and Liam O'Brien. He has imported from Dundalk his coach Noel King and Dermot Keely and from Hearts in Scotland Pat Byrne as skipper. They have between them created in a matter of months a side that is not just successful but successful in the Rovers tradition. Thus a team to match the lovely stadium at Glenmalure. Thus a part of what we used to be might be redeemed. Thus most importantly it is established that the country's premier league is no longer the playground of shabby impostors, but an acceptable facsimile of the Glory Game we dream about.

Epilogue
The Great Rovers Revival happened. But it made no difference. Time had moved on, we were in another age, the age of television. And it was over. Rover's success in the 80s proved that the world *does* change, some things die and can never be reincarnated.

Jim McLaughlin won 4 League of Ireland championships and 3 FAI cups. As far as cups and medals went you couldn't have asked for more. Sadly, cups and medals are not really what football is truly about. The game is about magic. These days magic comes from the box in the corner of your livingroom. It comes from Jack Charlton and his Irish soccer team with which we are now familiar, as indeed we are with the game in Britain.

The more Shamrock Rovers won in the 80s the fewer people went. The League of Ireland was dead. Part of the reason was that we had grown up. The most important change was, however, rooted in reality; football reality and the changing culture of our time. The sporting reality is that soccer is a street game. All the great players, the Coads, Touhys, McCanns and Mickey Bourkes learnt to weave magic on the streets. Kids don't play soccer on the streets anymore. They watch videos, go to McDonalds for their birthdays and have their own computers. They don't have to invent or improvise the way we used to in the bad old 50s. The consequence is that the magicians aren't bred anymore. The game has died or at least is dying. Old assumptions no longer hold, beauty now means something different.

Glenmalure Park is full of houses today. Mock something or other. You can never take culture for granted. Enjoy it while you can. The wonder that was Rovers is a memory now, something to cherish, from our childhood. A part of Dublin has vanished. Tomorrow's memories will be of Big Jack and "Iddly", Maradona and Captain Fantastic. Of High Germany, what it was like to watch the great matches. On television. It won't be the same. Perhaps it will be just as good. Perhaps. But it will never be majestic, nor as real as our fantastic journeys on the CIE Football Specials.

THE NEED TO BE ORDINARY
Eavan Boland

I am Chardin's woman,
edged in reflected light,
hardened by
the need to be ordinary.
(Self-Portrait on a Summer Evening)

There is a duality to place. There is the actual place which existed before you and will continue after you have gone. For the purpose of this piece, the actual place is Dundrum. I have lived here for eighteen of my forty-three years; longer, in fact than I have lived in any other one environment. But to say this is a piece about Dundrum, a South suburb of Dublin, would be misleading. There is the place that happened and the place that happens to you. And there are times - in work, in perception, in experience - when they are hard to disentangle from one another. At such times the inward adventure can become so enmeshed with the outward continuum that we live, not in one or the other, but at the point of intersection.

I suspect this piece is about just such an intersection. It is, of course, a particular version of a particular locale. But there may well be a more general truth disguised in it: that what we call place is really only that detail of it which we understand to be ourselves. "That's my Middle West" writes Fitzgerald in *The Great Gatsby* "not the wheat or the prairies or the lost Swede towns but the thrilling returning trains of my youth and the streetlamps and sleigh bells in the frosty dark and the shadows of holly wreaths thrown by lighted windows on the snow. I am part of that."

Questions of place were far from my mind that first winter, the second of our marriage, when we moved out here. We unpacked our books, put up our shelves and looked doubtfully at the raw floors and white walls of a new house. From the upstairs window we saw little to console us. Dundrum at this time, in the early seventies, was already starting to wander out to the foothills of the Dublin mountains. On those winter nights, in the first weeks of January, we learned to look for the lamps on the hills after dark; yellow and welcome as nocturnal crocuses.

For all that we were disoriented. I, at least, was thoroughly urban. The Dublin I had known until then was a sympathetic prospect of stone and water and wet dusks over Stephen's Green. It was a convivial town of coffee and endlessly renewable talk. I knew nothing of the city of contingencies. Now here it was, visible and oppressive, and still at a distance from the love I would come to feel for it.

The road outside our window was only half-laid. The house next door was built and the houses opposite were finished. There was good progress about half-way down our road. Walls were up, roofs were on, gardens were rotovated and, in some cases, even seeded. After about seven houses, however, the prospect gave out into mud and rubble. On a cold day it all seemed incomplete and improbable.

Now, on a summer morning, when the whitebeams are so thick they almost obscure the mimicking greens and greys of the mountains, I look back to that time and think of place as revelation.

That first spring, however, I thought of little else but practicalities. Ovens and telephones became images and emblems of the real world. The house was cold. We had no curtains. At night, the lights on the hills furnished the upper rooms with a motif of adventure and estrangement. In the morning the hills marched in, close or distant, promising rain or the dry breezes of a March day.

Now I find myself wishing that I had less of a sense of locale and more of local history. It was all to easy to allow a day to come down to the detail of a fabric or the weight of a chicken.

If I had looked about me with a wider sense of curiousity I would have noticed more. To start with, I would have seen a past as well as a present. I was oblivious, for instance, to the fact that Dundrum had its roots in Anglo-Norman times, when the castle had first been built to ward off the Wicklow clans. Its destiny as a residential centre had been settled centuries later, when the Harcourt Street railway line was opened. With its assistance the distance between Dundrum and the city centre became a mere sixteen miles.

It was all changing by the time we arrived. Indeed the arrival of young couples like ourselves was a signal of that change. But enough distinction remained to give a sense of the grace and equilibrium of the place it had been. Granted, the farriers at the corner of the village had been gone some twenty years. But the cobbler remained. Further down, the experiment of a mink farm had failed and a shopping centre was in the process of replacing it. Above all, the location remained: the wonderful poise of the village at the edge of the theatrical, wooded cliffs on the back road to Bray and under the incline of the Dublin mountains.

Occasionally I would become aware of the special contradictions and energies in our environment. More often I obscured it by seeing it through the lens of some small, practical crisis. Above all, I missed the vital inference: that the new shops, the traffic, the lights on the hills growing more numerous every year and we ourselves, were not isolated pieces of information. They and we were part of a pattern; one that was being repeated throughout Ireland in those years. Before our eyes, and because of them, a village was turning into a suburb.

I had lived in cities all my life. I made a distinction between a city you loved and a city you submitted to. I had not loved London, for instance, where I had spent the greater part of my childhood. The iron and gutted stone of its post-war prospect had seemed to me merely hostile. I was not won over by its parks, nor the scarlet truculence of its buses which carried me

161

forwards and backwards from school. Those were the early Fifties. I learned quickly, by inference at school and reference at home, that the Irish were unwelcome in London. I absorbed enough of that information to regard everything, even the jittery gleam from the breastplates of the Horseguards, as they rode through the city, with a sort of churlish inattention. All I knew, all I needed to know, was that none of this was mine.

New York was a different matter. The noise and speed of it persuaded me to try again. I was just twelve when I went there. I liked putting on skates in winter and shorts in summer. I had never known extremes, whether of dress or season, before. Now, on the edge of puberty, I responded to their drama.

Then there was Dublin. By the time I came to know it, those other cities had prepared me to relish a place which had something of the theatre of a city, and all the intimacy of a town. These were the early Sixties. There were still coffee bars set into the basements of Georgian houses, where a turf fire burned from four-o-clock in the afternoon and you could get brown scones with your coffee.

None of it prepared me for a suburb. There is, after all, a necessity about cities. By the time you come to them, their is something finished and inevitable about their architecture; even about their grime. You accept both.

A suburb is altogether more fragile and transitory. In one year it can seem a whole road is full of bicycles, roller skates, jumble sales. Garages will be wide-open with children selling comics and out-of-date raisin buns. There will be shouting and calling far into the summer night. Almost as soon, it seems, the same road will be quiet. The bicycles will be gone. The shouting and laughing will be replaced by one or two dogs barking in the back gardens. Curtains will be drawn till late morning and doors will stay closed.

The main feature about such quick and even violent transition is that it demands participants, not just witnesses. A suburb is made of lives in a state of process. "There is properly no history; only biography" wrote Emerson. To look down our road at lunchtime on a schoolday was to realize the force of his words. The public calendar defines a city; banks are shut and shops are opened. But the private one shapes a suburb. It waxes and wanes on christenings, weddings, funerals.

I found this potent mix everywhere in Dundrum. Obviously, it was a place with inevitabilities and schedules. There were buildings, shops and visible progresses to prove it. But it was the hidden history that drew me. I had missed this before. I knew too little of the countryside to find it there; I recoiled too much from cities to search for it in them. But here, in my own home, on my own road, the private history which is to be found in the unique transaction between a life and a place began to unfold in front of me.

And where does poetry come in? Without a doubt, there were summer dusks and clear, vacant winter mornings when I was certain this place nurtured my poetry. I might have found it hard to say how or why. In all seasons, at all times, the suburb gathered around me and filled my immediate distance. At times it could be a shelter; it was never a cloister. Everywhere you looked there were reminders - a child's bicycle thrown sideways on the grass, a single roller skate, a tree in its first April of blossom - that lives were not lived here in any sort of static pageant; but that they thrived, waned, changed, began and ended here.

Inevitably, this sense of growth could not remain just at the edge of things. Apart from anything else, time was passing. Roads were laid. Houses were finished. The builders moved out. Summers came and went and trees began to define the road. Garden walls were put up and soon enough the voices calling over them on long, bright evenings, the bicycle thrown on its side and the single roller skate belonged to my children. Somewhat to my surprise, I had done what most human beings have done. I had found a world and I had populated it. In so doing, my imagination had been radically stirred and redirected. It was not, of course, a simple process. In poetry, let alone in life, it never is. It would be wrong, even now, to say that my poetry expressed the suburb. The more accurate version is that my poetry allowed me to experience it. And the more I experienced it, the more the distinction between its literal outline and its imaginative meaning became unclear.

At what point does an actual, exact landscape - those details which are recurrent and predictable - begin to blur and soften? Sometimes on a summer evening, walking between my house and a neighbour's, past the whitebeam trees and the bicycles left glinting in the dusk, I could imagine that I myself was a surreal and changing outline; that there was something almost profound in these reliable shadows; that such lives like mine and my neighbours' were mythic, not because of their strangeness but because of their powerful ordinariness. When I reached a point in the road where I could see the children at the end of it, milling around, shrieking in the consciousness that they would have to come in soon, I would stand there with my hand sickle-shaped to my eyes. Almost always I was just trying to remember which cotton T-shirt one child of mine or the other was wearing so I could pick it out in the summer twilight and go and scoop them up and bring them in. But just occasionally, standing and breathing in the heavy musks of rose-beds and buddleias, I would feel an older and less temporary connection to the moment. Then I would feel all the sweet, unliterate melancholy of women who must have stood as I did, throughout continents and centuries, feeling the timelessness of that particular instant and the cruel time underneath its surface. They must have measured their children, as I did, against the seasons; and looked at the hedges and rowan trees, their height and the colour of their berries, as an index of the coming loss.

Is it true, as Patrick Kavanagh says, in his beautiful poem "Epic", that "gods make their own importance"? Is the origin, in other words, so restless in the outcome that the parish, the homestead, the place is a powerful source as well as a practical location? On such evenings, if my thoughts had not been full of details and children, I could have wondered where myth begins. Is it in the fears for harvest and the need for rain? Are its roots in the desire to make the strange familiar, to domesticate the thunder and give a shape to the frost? Or does it have, as Kavanagh argues, a more local and ritual source? Is there something about the repeated action - about lifting a child, clearing a dish, watching the seasons return to a tree and depart from a vista - which reveals a deeper meaning to existence and heals some of the worst abrasions of time?

Not suddenly then, but definitely and gradually, a place I lived became a country of the mind. Perhaps anywhere I had grown used to, raised my children in, written my poetry about, would have become this. But a suburb by its very nature - by its hand-to-mouth compromises between town and country - was particularly well suited to the transformation. Looking out my window at familiar things I could realize that there had always been something compromised in my own relation to places. They had never been permanent. Therefore I had never developed a stable perception about them.

Now here at last was permanence, an illusory permanence, of course. But enough stability to make me realize that the deepest sustenances are not in the new or surprising. And with that realization came the surrender of any prospect of loving new things; a prospect so vital when I was younger. I no longer felt like Martial, who advocated the value of rarity: "greater charm" he wrote "belongs to early apples and winter roses". Instead, many of the things I now did - from the casual gesture of looking out a window to the writing of poems - became an act of possessing the old things in a new way. I watched for the return of the magpies, every February, to their nest in the poplars just beyond my garden. I took an almost concert-hall pleasure, in an August twilight, in listening to the sound of my neighbours' shears as she cut and pruned and made things ready for another season. It seemed to me, for instance, a small but definite drama when the rowan tree in our front garden blew down in a storm. It was a young tree, planted when we moved into the house. Its berries, at the end of each summer, marked the beginnings of other things: school uniforms, the tang of new weather, the incarnation of different routines. When it lay broken on the front grass, a casualty of our exposed position, it took on the pity and symmetry of a small metaphor. When it was staked back to the ground with a metal pole, and somehow, with this unglamorous support, began to thrive again, the metaphor brightened and intensified.

None of this was purely instinctive; none of it involved an intellectual suppression or simplification. Indeed, I had a clearer sense, as time went on, of the meaning of all this to me as a poet. I knew what repetitions meant in poetry.

I understood those values in language and restraint. When Coleridge wrote, in the Biographia Literaria, of metrical units as "at first the offspring of passion and then the adopted children of power" I felt I understood a concept of linguistic patterning, which both lulled the mind and facilitated the meaning.

Now here, in front of me every day, were repetitions which had almost exactly the same effect. The crocuses under the rowan tree. The same child, wheeled down to the shops at the same time every day. A car that returned home, with the identical dinge on its bumper, every night. And the lamps which sprang into symmetries across our hills at dusk in November. What were all these if not - as language and music in poetry are - a sequence and repetition which allowed the deeper meanings to emerge: a sense of belonging, of sustenance; of a life revealed, and not restrained, by ritual and patterning?

Place itself is not a metaphor. It would be reductive to see a busy neighbourhood with all its transitions and necessities as metaphorical. What I have tried to write about here is neither metaphorical nor emblematic; but something which is, in fact, the common source of both. There is a quality about the minute changes, the gradations of a hedge, the small growth of a small boy, which makes a potent image out of an ordinary day in a suburb. Nothing I have described here can catch the simple force for me of looking out my window on one of those mornings at the end of winter, when a few small, burgandy rags would be on the wild cherry tree; but otherwise everything was bare and possessed a muted sort of expectancy. The hills would have the staring blues which signalled rain. A car would pass by. A neighbour's dog would bark, and then be silent. Maybe the daffodils which had been closed the week before would now be open, after an afternoon of that quick, buttery sunshine which is the best part of an Irish spring. I would lean out the window of the children's room, which faced directly towards the mountains. And I would know exactly what Cezanne had meant when he wrote of Provence: "I think I could occupy myself for months," he stated, in a letter to his son "without changing my place, simply bending a little more to left or right".

Of course, I did not look at the place I lived, day after day, with the sacramental vision of a painter. More often than not, the wonderful relation of routine to ritual, ritual to rite, and rite to metaphor was obscured by the hand-to mouth practicalities of daily living. Often enough I went to the side window and looked out, and not to see the whitebeams or the lamplight, but just to make sure the frost was not too heavy to make the roads slippery for the school run in the morning. There were many days, perhaps the majority of them, when I was bad company for the inward adventure I had stumbled on. A child might be sick. I might have a heavy workload of lectures or paperwork. Then I was oblivious to the slight creeping of colour into the landscape, the sounds of laughter and shrieking down in the Square, which grew later with the daylight. But always, the place found me again. Always, I wanted to be found.

Dundrum April 1988

DUN-LAOGHAIRE, DUN-LEARY
Conleth O'Connor

Being born in 1947 meant that I escaped the Second World War but it also meant that I was too early for most of the benefits inherent in the alleged economic boom of the Sixties with its attendent freedoms.

However, too many people spend their time thinking about their futures while ignoring life as it is in the present. Consequently, they run the risk of ending up with little or no memories or cluttered with inaccuracies to argue over in later life.

Dun-Laoghaire or Kingstown as I heard it referred to on a number of occasions is a kind of geographical and social cul-de-sac. It is famous for its harbour and its small boats. It also boasts some worthwhile architectural features, some reasonable housing and a population of local council tenants far larger than one realises. To abide by the media pundits one would have thought that the only County Council or Local Housing estates in the city and suburbs of Dublin were to be found in Ballyfermot, Finglas or Tallaght. Few seemed to want to acknowledge the existence of Sallynoggin or Monkstown Farm.

The house I lived in had three storeys, one of 15 in a square that cossetted a hockey ground from the winds and weather. The houses on both sides of Royal Terrace (shades of past glories or pretensions?) were at the time, mostly owner occupied with a sprinkling of commercial Guest Houses. In summer, North of England and Scottish visitors of the middle aged, floral printed dressed women and potbellied men variety, inhabited these places for their annual holidays. The younger crowd went further up the coast to Bray. A great number of the larger houses in the various other squares plied a similar trade during the "season". In winter a few stayed open for their regulars (teachers at local schools, bank officials and other transients). The only real impression the summer visitors left me was the sound of their accents which as kids we used to mimic at every opportunity and the ability to recognise the species as players, and members of the audience in television games and chat shows from BBC and ITV.

The hockey ground is the home turf of Monkstown Hockey Club. This game is played mainly by Protestants for Protestants and every saturday during the season you could hear the Argues, Smyths, Murdocks et al, urged on by shouts of "Come Awwn Tow-On, Come Awwn Tow-On", as they bullied on with the sporting elevens of Three Rock Rovers, Palmerstown and Trinity College, among others.

I never played hockey. But, I can remember being removed from the ground by the police who used to take our names on a regular basis. A neighbour (known to us) used to ring the local gardai anytime we ventured onto the "sacred turf" wielding a hurley or kicking a round football. For some odd reason we were left undisturbed if playing cricket (which I did) or kicking an oval ball (which I didn't). Seemingly, prejudice is also in the eye of the beholder.

It was sometime around the age of 12 that I had my first cigarette. White, Kingsized, tipped in a red packet (not an inappropriate name consideration?). Myself and Paul Singer, son of Dr. Paul Singer of Shanahan Stamp Auction fame. They cost 11 old pence for 10. After one fag the pair of us vomited the remains of at least that day's meals against a telephone pole at the back of the last house in Royal Terrace West.

While on the subject of smoke it's not everybody in the South of Ireland who has the opportunity of witnessing a church being burned and gutted. I can still remember the glee with which I watched St Michael's Catholic Church in Dun Laoghaire enflamed in 1964 and the pleasure I derived from passing on the news to family and friends. However, it wasn't until later that I fully understood my reactions to the event.

The Mail Boats, the Leinster and the infamous St. Maude

were a great source of pleasure and curiosity. The boat trains full of country people on the emigration trail. I had to wait until I was a great deal older and sitting in the Abbey at some stage-Irish crap, to see an echo of the scenes enacted out around the East Pier in Dun-Laoghaire. As a nation we seemed to care little for our young and not so young who were whisked away. Dun-Laoghaire itself and its Borough councils manifested the country's shame by refusing even the meagrest of facilities for those departing. There was no place to rest. Not even a simple tea-room. It seemed as if these embarrassments were to be got rid of quickly, silently, discreetly. It's no wonder sometimes when I gaze at the twin piers attempting to meet and the present day car ferries slipping out through the gap between them, that I think of Dun-Laoghaire as the arse of Ireland, functioning regularly.

Money didn't seem to be much of an issue, at least during the summer. The sea and swimming kept us occupied all day and often into the late evening. In good weather, we would start early in the morning at Seapoint, work our way during the day to the baths and finish after tea at the 40 foot. To-day, the seashore is polluted, the baths annually run the risk of closure. I certainly wouldn't allow my nine year old son, Breffni, to wander away for such long periods to the places described. The contemporary problems alluded to and the lack of any evidence to suggest any decrease in the population of child molesters, flashers and others condemn him to swimming in a heated pool at an appointed time on a specific day for limited duration. It leaves me to speculate on the retreat of the word freedom back into the dictionary.

The few bob did become important when in later years we discovered snooker in Frank's place, situated neatly between the Labour Exchange and within a few hundred yards of a bookie's shop. It was there we enhanced our vocabularly and learned to lose real money at games such as pool. Consequently, our visits to the No.1 and No.2 tables were few and chastening, unless of course on the days of Big races, Derby Day for instance when the regulars vacated the premises for the bookies. I played endless rubbers with a school friend and on a Sunday night the loser had to pay for the table.

The 60s were well into their stride and I can only agree with the TV personality (apologies for not remembering his name) who said that they were a long party that he hadn't been invited to. After school and at the week-ends we sat in the Bamboo Cafe (now defunct), drank coffee, were idealistic and got high on alleged hash that some chancer used to make up with a combination of Light Shag and Balkan Sobranie tobaccos wrapped in Rizla papers - liquorice type. It was time to head for the hills and I did. I joined An Oige.

When not scouring the countryside at the week-ends the biggest attraction was the local dance on Saturday night. A few pints of Guinness in one of the local hotel lounges, the 46A to Stradbrook, a short frenzied walk to the hall for a night of, among others, Tina and The Mexicans. It was there I met *Woman*. My youth was over and so were the sixties.

GROWING UP IN GLASTHULE
Joe Jackson

Ride the rails all the way from Westland Row to Bray and you'll see no official acknowledgement of the existence of a track-side village that is home to roughly 3,000 people. *That* fact alone surely qualifies Glasthule for the title of numero uno "invisible suburb" on, at least, the southside of Dublin city, right? The name used to have pride of place alongside "Sandycove" at our local train station but that was before the Dart accelerated the creeping "yuppification" of the area. Perhaps "Glasthule" had to go because it sounds just a wee bit *plebian*, and, as such, makes a mockery of the highly-marketable lie that there are no working class communities at all "Southside", who knows?

And perhaps only a "pleb" like myself would expect a station situated *in* Glasthule, to bear the area's name and *not* relinquish its territorial identity to one of its nearest neighbours. Even if the more "refined" Sandycove did give us Roger Casement and was home, for a moment or three, to that collosus of literature: James Joyce. "Key figures in the political and cultural landscape" as my father used to say, quite proudly. Yet during some of our more surreal discussions about "Ulysses" he joked about what might have happened if Joyce had taken a wrong turn when he originally stepped out of Glasthule/Sandycove station. "Imagine. The greatest novel in the world could have opened with a description of your granny, in a yellow dressing gown, holding a bowl on high and intoning *Introibi ad altare Dei,*" he'd laugh, fracturing the latin with his self-educated labourer's tongue. Yet still echoing all these years after my father's death is the question "*would* Joyce have found anything else to celebrate if he'd stayed in Glasthule, rather than moved up the road, and upmarket, to

Sandycove?" I suspect so. Particularly if he'd grown up in the area.

This is not to suggest that Glasthule always had pride-of-place in my heart. On the contrary. At times growing up here proved to be a pain in the arse. Especially on those wet Saturday afternoons in the early 60s when, as a boy of twelve or so, I'd be queueing up outside the Dun Laoghaire Adelphi, waiting to see the latest Elvis movie. "Barnsie", one of the ushers, would systematically prod bodies apart with the handle of his silver flashlight all the while grumbling "Are *you* from the holla? Everyone from the holla is barred." Living, as I did then, on the layers of sex, sun, song and the overall sense of escapism that was available via Elvis movies like "Fun in Acapulco" I learned to fib, to deny my roots, say "No, Mr. Barnes, I'm from Sandycove." A shameful denial, I now realise, yet it was a trick I'd been taught at the local C.B.S. where a brother once told me "Jackson, when you're old enough to apply for a job, *never* admit you're from Glasthule, write Eden Villas, *Sandycove*, instead."

But then my time in the Dun Laoghaire C.B.S. had begun with questions being raised, at a parents'-teachers' meeting, about how a boy from Glasthule had infiltrated his way into the school ahead of so many more "suitable students" from areas such as Dalkey and Killiney. Wasn't my "type" supposed to attend Glasthule's Harolds National School, it was argued. And indeed we were. Yet my parents, through what they later revealed were "connections" had seen to it that I'd never gone to the local "redbrick university" and I became one of the only four families in our 101-house corporation estate whose sons "graduated" to the C.B.S. Both my mother and father were quite painfully aware that "the holla" was a dip in the land between Dun Laoghaire and Dalkey into which most people had originally been poured in order to service the local factories and various "lords and ladies" of the many middle-upper class manors nearby. True to this socio-political dictate my father, at the time, was working for a Sandycove builder, and my mother cleaned what my sister and I described as a

174

"mansion" in Foxrock, two mornings a week. However, they were determined that their children would one day burst beyond these boundaries.

Meanwhile, back in the tarmacadamed schoolyard those infinitely "more suitable students" from lyrically named locations like Killiney found highly amusing the fact that anyone could live in a place called "Glasthule". Even they were aware that "tool" was a slang word for penis and so the predictable jibes were "Can you see through yours?" and, the more popular, "If you're from glass-tool you must have relatives in still-organ!" As sophisticated and funny as the latter line was, at the time all it led to was a smack in the gob of the snob who'd delivered the jibe and a blur of Christian Brothers' uniforms, sometimes bloodied, rolling round the schoolyard, or slamming against doors in the loo.

Unfortunately, my peers in Eden Villas, knew nothing of the proud stand I was taking for our neighbourhood, as the fact that I hadn't gone to the local "redbrick university" and was forbidden, by my father, "to mix with them in any way" meant that they assumed I too was "a bit of a snob". The net result of this was that for a time I became target number one when guerilla, if not class-warfare, would break out near the Eden Road bridge as I'd head back to school at lunch-hour. Red berries would be spit from bamboo shoots, a stone would be thrown in retaliation and then face to face combat would begin. Having been trained in the fine art of street fighting by my father and having gone, for a short period, to Sallynoggin Boxing Club, one-to-one I'd usually win. However, cornered by a gang that included the magnificently named "Mimmer" Merrigan, "Monty Mooney", "Mousey" Hanlon, "Dippy" O'Connor and the Duffy's I'd have the shit beaten out of me. My opponents sometimes proved themselves to be mean-spirited little bastards at the time too. Stealing, on St. Stephen's day, the new bike I'd been given for Christmas and dropping it, sans wheels, onto the local railway-line and, at one point, dragging me along the ground to tear the knees out of my much-envied, first long trouser'd suit. Needless to say, I was

175

not developing a strong sense of belonging to any class, or community, a feeling that has persisted to this day.

However, this dominant sense of separateness was softened considerably in 1964 when I became a member of St. Brendan's Boys' Club, *the* centre-of-the-universe for most young boys growing up in Glasthule at the time. Former opponents like the two Ken's, Duffy and Hanlon, became tentative friends. And true, lasting relationships were formed with fellow social misfits such as Paul English. Just as importantly "the club" *was* a bonded community which, along with an entire generation of young people in '64, was beginning to loudly celebrate a new form of popular culture, a culture that was predominantly working class. Nowhere was this more in evidence than during my first "club holiday" in Gormanston, Co. Meath, where, despite my increasingly alienating allegience to Elvis and my hidden anger at the fact that his "throne" was being threatened by the "fab, four mop-heads from Liverpool" I too, like everyone else, bought the Beatle bubblegum, wore a Lennon cap and learned "off by heart" every track from "A Hard Day's Night". And later, back from the holiday, when a group of us were singing the aggressive "You Can't Do That" outside the local chipper, I *just knew* we'd mastered the Liverpool accents in a way that could never be equalled by my schoolmates from Killiney, no matter how hard they tried. Later again I went back to school and the suitably nicknamed "Lofty", a maths teacher, said "Jackson, have you given up following Elvis and gone over to The Beatles?" I hadn't, of course, but the new, fringed hairstyle which had replaced my by-then anachronistic "G.I. Blues" crewcut, was a sign that I'd been integrated, to a degree, into my own community and had discovered a sense of confidence in style, a look, a way of talking that seemed to be peculiarly *ours*. I also discovered the heretofore unexplored delights of growing up in Glasthule.

Such as? There were seemingly endless bonfires and sing-songs "on the bank" of the railway-line, expeditions over the wall of Glengara Boarding School to try catch a glimpse of schoolgirls undressing, then back to the fire to hear tales of the local "pro" who had the good grace to have her place of residence within reach of the statue of the Virgin Mary which was situated in the centre of Eden Villas. But most exciting of all, in 1965, was climbing into the ventilation area in the roof of "Club Caroline" and actually seeing *in-person,* a real-live rock 'n' roll band, The Animals, perform "House Of the Rising Sun". In *our* hometown! Though I must admit I enjoyed almost as much the gang-war near Joyce's Tower in Sandycove, where the older "Glasthulers" met and finally vanquished "the fancy boys from Sandier".

And so it continued throughout the halcyon summer of '65, with "the club" being the rallying point every Wednesday and Friday nights. However, despite the presence of visiting priests who would propagate the christian denial of all body areas below the waist and warn us that masturbation "will make you go blind" some boys were undoubtedly discovering the first rush of teenage passion as they rallied round the bushes at the back of the club-house. Older boys had tried to grope my balls once or twice and, in a mock fight, one had tried to force himself upon me, quite violently. Yet if I'd gone through the normal homosexual phase in my early teens it had been discharged, on an unconscious level, through Elvis Presley. Consciously, my mind and potentially self-blinding fantasies, were very much filled with images of Elvis' co-stars, such as Ursula Andress, Ann Margret and Jocelyn Lane. Besides, in 1965, as Dun Laoghaire Church, situated across the road from the C.B.S. was being gutted by fire, I was rushing to defy priests and brothers and descend into my own form of heavenly hell by indulging in my first *serious* "wearing-session" nearby, with Doris, from Blackrock. A young girl's screaming "Elvis, you're a big ride" a year beforehand, in the Adelphi, had finally cracked any chance of Catholicism exerting too strong a hold over my sexuality. That summer ended with my again trembling-knee-deep in a "heavy petting session" though this time with my first "real girlfriend", Deirdre. Symbolically, again, we'd meet and hide behind a wall in the shadows of

177

Glasthule's "Chapel Lane". If Jesus was frowning I didn't give a damn. Nor was I too disturbed by the fact that the entrance of girls into my life had put the first, irreconcilable strains on the "gang" I'd been part of in Glasthule. The pattern was set, which would be repeated for the rest of the 60s. If not, in ways, for the rest of my life.

By 1969 I'd passed the cut-off age of 16 and was supposed to leave St. Brendan's Youth Club, as it had since become. In ways I wanted to because, for the first time in five years, I'd found more exciting ways of spending my Wednesdays, Fridays and most nights of the week, with my latest girlfriend, Phyll. We'd even begun to use those stained bushes at the back of the clubhouse in order to play our own little games. Yet still I secretly cried at the thought of finally closing the door on an experience that had, in many ways, defined my adolescence. For a time I became "resident D.J." and, what one brother described as "Pied Piper" to a group of "juniors" as I led them on a merry march around the table tennis area and in and out of the billiard room, with sweeping brushes nestled in their shoulders, and all in time to Elvis' singing "He's Your Uncle, Not Your Dad". It was a tentative last link to those days of innocence yet 22 years later I'm still asked by my ageing recruits if I remember that specific song and the joy of those evenings in the club. At times I suspect I will forever chase even a fleeting facsimile of those feelings.

However, as the decade ended I, and all the original gang-members, had left the club. I'd also finally moved back "downmarket" from the secondary to the local "tech" and was seemingly set to follow the patterns my parents had wanted so much for me to break. I was serving my time as an apprentice sheetmetalworker, servicing the factory of a man who, ironically enough, had once lived in "the holla" yet now owned a "mansion" on Dalkey Hill. Yet despite the endless years of factory life that were laid out before me I secretly adopted as my theme song, Elvis', "If I Can Dream" and I held on to my deep-set longing to one day be accepted as a writer. It was a dream I'd inherited from my father. A dream he, tragically, never lived to see fulfilled.